YOGA FOR PEOPLE WHO CAN'T BE BOTHERED TO DO IT

Geoff Dyer is the author of *Jeff in Venice, Death in Varanasi* and three previous novels, as well as nine non-fiction books. Dyer has won the Somerset Maugham Prize, the Bollinger Everyman Wodehouse Prize for Comic Fiction, a Lannan Literary Award, the International Center of Photography's 2006 Infinity Award for writing on photography and the American Academy of Arts and Letters' E.M. Forster Award. In 2009 he was named *GQ*'s Writer of the Year. He won a National Book Critics Circle Award in 2012 and was a finalist in 1998. His books have been translated into more than twenty languages. He lives in London.

geoffdyer.com

Also by Geoff Dyer

YOGA FOR PEOPLE WHO CAN'T BE BOTHERED TO DO IT

GEOFF DYER

CANONGATE

This paperback edition published in Great Britain in 2012 by
Canongate Books Ltd, 14 High Street, Edinburgh EH1 1TE

canongate.co.uk

4

First published in the United States in 2003 by Pantheon Books.
First published in Great Britain in 2003 by Abacus,
an imprint of Little, Brown Book Group,
100 Victoria Embankment, London EC4Y 0DY

Portions of this book originally appeared in *Fortune Hotel*, edited
by Sarah Champion (Hamish Hamilton, 1999); *New Writing 10*, edited
George Szirtes and Penelope Lively (Picador, 2001);
All Hail the New Puritans, edited by Nicholas Blincoe and Matt Thorne (4th
Estate, 2000); *Feed*; and *Modern Painters*.

British Library Cataloguing-in-Publication Data
A catalogue record for this book is available on
request from the British Library

ISBN 978 0 85786 406 2

Typeset in Goudy Old Style by Palimpsest Book Production Ltd,
Falkirk, Stirlingshire

Printed and bound in Great Britain by Clays Ltd, Elcograf S.p.A.

For Rebecca

Everything is unique, nothing happens more than once in a lifetime. The physical pleasure which a certain woman gave you at a certain moment, the exquisite dish which you ate on a certain day – you will never meet either again. Nothing is repeated, and everything is unparalleled.

THE GONCOURT BROTHERS

. . . and this moonlight between the trees, and even this moment and I myself.

NIETZSCHE

CONTENTS

For several years now I've been puzzled by some lines of Auden's – actually, I've been puzzled by many of Auden's lines, but the ones I have in mind are from 'Detective Story' (1936), where he talks about

> home, the centre where the three or four things
> That happen to a man do happen

I think I have trouble getting my head round this idea of home because I can't refine down the number of things that have happened to me to 'three or four' – or not yet I can't anyway. Auden might turn out to be right, but for the moment, there are a lot of things that have happened, and they've happened in lots of different places. 'Home', by contrast, is the place where least has happened. For the last dozen or so years, in fact, the idea of 'home' has felt peripheral and, as a consequence, more than a little blurred. Or maybe, like Steinbeck, 'I have homes everywhere', many of which 'I have not seen yet. That is perhaps why I am restless. I haven't seen all my homes.'

Auden's poem begins with the question 'Who is ever

quite without his landscape . . . ?' Halfway through the first stanza he asks, 'Who cannot draw the map of his life . . . ?' I can't (or can't yet). This book is a ripped, by no means reliable map of some of the landscapes that make up a particular phase of my life. It's about places where things happened or didn't happen, places where I stayed and things that have stayed with me, places I'd wanted to see or places I passed through or just ended up. In a way they're all the same place – the same landscape – because the person these things happened to was the same person who in turn is the sum of all the things that happened or didn't happen in these and other places. Everything in this book really happened, but some of the things that happened only happened in my head; by the same token, all the things that didn't happen didn't happen there too.

HORIZONTAL DRIFT

In 1991 I lived for a while in New Orleans, in an apartment on Esplanade, just beyond the French Quarter, where from time to time British tourists are murdered for refusing to hand over their video cameras to the cracked-out muggers who live and work near by. I never had any trouble – I've never owned a video camera, either – even though I walked everywhere at all times.

I'd decided to come to New Orleans after a girlfriend and I passed through, on our way to Los Angeles from New York. We were delivering a car, and though, usually, you are allowed only a few hundred miles more than it takes to drive cross-continent in a straight line, our car's original mileage had not been recorded, and so we zigzagged our way across the States, exceeding the normal distance by several thousand miles and thoroughly exhausting ourselves in the process. In the course of this frenzied itinerary we'd stayed only one night in New Orleans, but it – by which I mean the French Quarter rather than the city at large – seemed like the most perfect place in the world, and I vowed that when I next had a chunk of free time, I would return. I make such vows all the time without keeping them, but on this occasion, a year after first passing through, I returned to New Orleans to live for three months.

I spent the first few nights in the Rue Royal Inn while I looked for an apartment to rent. I hoped to find a place in the heart of the Quarter, somewhere with a balcony and rocking chairs and wind chimes, overlooking other places with rocking chairs and balconies, but I ended up on the dangerous fringes of the Quarter, in a place with a tiny balcony overlooking a vacant lot which seethed with unspecified threat as I walked home at night.

The only people I knew in New Orleans were James and Ian, a gay couple in their fifties, friends of an acquaintance of a woman I knew in London. They were extremely hospitable, but because they were a good deal older than I and because they both had AIDS and liked to live quietly, I settled quickly into a routine of work and solitude. In films, whenever a man moves to a new town – even if he has served a long jail term for murdering his wife – he soon meets a woman at the checkout of the local supermarket or at the diner where he has his first breakfast. I spent much of my thirties moving to new towns, towns where I knew no one, and I never met a woman in the supermarket or the Croissant d'Or, where I had breakfast on my first morning in New Orleans. Even though I did not meet a waitress at the aptly named Croissant d'Or, I continued to have breakfast there every day because they served the best almond croissants I had (and have) ever tasted. Some days it rained for days on end, the heaviest rain I had ever seen (I've seen worse since), but however hard it was raining I never missed my breakfast at the Croissant d'Or, partly because of the excellence of the croissants and coffee, but mainly because going there became part of the habitual rhythm of my day.

In the evenings I went to the bar across the road, the Port of Call, where I tried, unsuccessfully, to engage the barmaid in conversation while watching the Gulf War on CNN. On the night of the first air strikes against Baghdad, the bar was rowdy with excitement and foreboding. Yellow ribbons were tied around many of the trees on Esplanade, which I walked up every day on my way to the Croissant d'Or, where, as I ate my almond croissants, I liked to read the latest reports from the Gulf, either in the *New York Times* or in the local paper, whose name – the *Louisiana* something? – I have forgotten. After breakfast I walked home and worked for as long as I could, and then strolled through the Quarter, led on, it seemed, by the sound of wind chimes, which hung from almost every building. It was January but the weather was mild, and I often sat by the Mississippi reading about New Orleans and its history. Because the city is located at the mouth of the Mississippi, its foundations are in mud, and each year the buildings sink more deeply into it. As well as being warped by the sun and rotted by rain and humidity, many of the buildings in the Quarter sloped markedly as a result of subsidence. This straying from the vertical was complemented by a horizontal drift. The volume of detritus carried south by the Mississippi was such that the river was silting itself up and changing course so that, effectively, the city was moving. Every year the streets moved a fraction of an inch in relation to the river, subtly altering the geography of the town. Decatur Street, for example, where James and

Ian lived, had moved several degrees from the position recorded on nineteenth-century maps.

As I sat by the Mississippi one afternoon, a freight rumbled past on the railroad track behind me, moving very slowly. I'd always wanted to hop a freight, and I sprang up, trying to muster up the courage to leap aboard. The length of the train and its slow speed meant that I had a long time – too long – to contemplate hauling myself aboard, but I was frightened of getting into trouble or injuring myself, and I stood there for five minutes, watching the boxcars clank past, until finally there were no more carriages and the train had passed. Watching it curve out of sight, I was filled with magnolia-tinted regret, the kind of feeling you get when you see a woman in the street, when your eyes meet for a moment but you make no effort to speak to her and then she is gone and you spend the rest of the day thinking that, had you spoken, she would have been pleased, not offended, and you would, perhaps, have fallen in love with each other. You wonder what her name might have been. Angela perhaps. Instead of hopping the freight, I went back to my apartment on Esplanade and had the character in the novel I was working on do so.

When you are lonely, writing can keep you company. It is also a form of self-compensation, a way of making up for things – as opposed to making things up – that did not quite happen.

As the eventless weeks went by it became warmer and more humid, and Mardi Gras drew near. A condition of renting my apartment was that I move out during Mardi Gras, when it was possible to charge four or five times the normal weekly rate. Fortunately, James and Ian were going away and they allowed me to stay in their place on Decatur which was no longer quite as close to the river as it had once been. At first it was fun, Mardi Gras. I liked the sport of trying to catch stuff – plastic beakers, beads, and other trinkets, rubbish really – thrown from the crazy floats inching through the crowded streets. It was like a cross between basketball and being in a mob of refugees scrambling for food rations thrown by soldiers. Being tall, I could outreach most people, even though there are some tall men, mainly black, in Louisiana; the whites are shorter for the most part, easy to outjump. One night I was part of a herd buffaloing along Rampart, leaping for beakers and beads, when gunshots were heard. Suddenly everyone was screaming and we were all running in panic. For some reason – it had never happened before – one of my knees gave way and I lurched forward into the person ahead of me, would have fallen to the ground if I hadn't grabbed hold of him. This initiated another brief surge of panic, and then everyone stopped running and there were sirens and police everywhere and things returned to the normal Mardi Gras uproar.

As the carnival progressed so it became more unpleasant, almost a bore. The Quarter was jammed with college kids and tins of Budweiser and broken plastic beakers, and the streets reeked of old beer and fresh vomit. The flip side of this was the extravagant balls organized by various krewes. Ian had given me his invitation to one of these bashes, where I met Angela, a young black woman who was studying wealth accumulation at law school. The day after the ball she came round to James and Ian's apartment wearing freshly laundered Levi's and a red blouse. Her hair was tied back in a ribbon, also red. We stood side by side on the balcony, drinking white wine in glasses so fine you hardly dared hold them. Our hands on the balcony rail were only inches apart. I moved my hand until it almost touched hers, and then it was touching hers and she didn't move her hand away, so I stroked her arm.

'That feels nice,' she said, still looking out into the street. Then we kissed, each holding a delicate glass behind the other's back. Unsure what to do when we had finished kissing, we kissed some more.

Shortly after Mardi Gras, when the Quarter had returned to its quiet, empty norm, Donelly, a guy about my age and height, moved into the apartment next to mine. He had longish hair, dressed less smartly – T-shirt, baseball shoes – than I did at that time. We met on the stairs a couple of times, compared apartments – they were almost identical – and went for a burger at the Port of Call and started hanging out together. About four years ago – 'April Fool's Day 1987,' he said – Donelly had been told he had skin cancer. The doctors gave him only a 30/70 chance of living, but he had come through a series of operations sufficiently full of life to try, five months before we met, to kill himself. Since then he'd been in a mental home in LA, and was now 'undergoing' further cancer treatment at Tulane (hospitals, in Donelly's résumé, played the part of colleges in mine).

Being from California, Donelly was a good tennis player, and in the afternoons we often knocked up for an hour (he couldn't see the point in keeping score). He was a much better player than I, but since I enjoyed running down every ball and was possessed of a fierce determination to win (even though we weren't scoring), we were perfectly matched. When he took off his sweat-soaked T-shirt at the end of our first game I was shocked by the state of his back and chest: a mass of scarred and maimed flesh. In the evenings we got stoned or hung out in bars, usually the Port of Call, sometimes other places. He was always happy to talk about 'the cancer and shit' he'd been through. He'd been living at his parents' house when the first test results came back positive.

'I was in the bathroom, shaving. My mom opened the envelope and came in and hugged me. I'm like, "Mom, I'm *shaving*."'

'You were never upset?'

'It fucked up my life but I wasn't upset. You know, they kept talking about "undergoing" surgery, "undergoing" chemo. It really bugged me. I never saw it that way. I was just living my life. I wasn't "undergoing" it.'

We were sitting on my balcony when he told me this, watching kids playing in the vacant lot. It was growing dark quickly.

'So why'd you try to kill yourself?' I asked.

'It wasn't like I was depressed or anything. I didn't even want to die particularly. I just didn't want to live any more.' He'd been doing coke all night, he said. Then he sat in his car drinking beer, playing tapes, quite happy, a tube from the exhaust filling the interior with carbon monoxide.

It was dark now, still warm. We could no longer see the kids playing, but we could hear their voices.

'What did your friends think?' I said.

'I think they thought, That's just like Donelly.'

The doctors at the mental home were no less intrigued than I was. They had encountered many attempted suicides but had never come across a case like his. Searching for clues, they asked if he was 'possibly an alcoholic?'

'I should hope so,' he said. 'After all the time, money and effort I've put into it.'

Nothing made any difference to him. He didn't care about anything, and yet, at the same time, he had a great capacity for friendship. He was thoughtful, generous (he wasn't working but he always had plenty of money), never imposing, but eager to come along whenever I suggested we go for a drink or something to eat. If ever I knocked on his door, he was always lying on his bed, drinking beer or watching TV. He never read anything – not even newspapers – and he was never bored. He spent all his time being himself, being American, being Donelly.

On a weekend when Donelly's family were visiting, Angela and I drove to Mississippi in her car. She had been away for a time, staying with friends on the East Coast, and we had not seen each other for several weeks. Also, although we had necked a lot, we had never quite slept together. I hoped that would happen in the course of what I referred to as our 'freedom ride'. Angela did not know what I meant. This was ten years ago; back then I was constantly surprised by how much people didn't know. That's one of the things about travelling, one of the things you learn: many people in the world, even educated ones, don't know much, and it doesn't actually matter at all.

We drove through the flatness of Louisiana, past Walker Evans scenery and lots of poor housing, which became poorer as we got into Mississippi. If we were driving slowly people stopped what they were doing – even if they were doing nothing – and watched us pass. The sky was heavy and wet, silted with cloud. I was vaguely hoping that we would be subjected to racial abuse, that a redneck in a baseball cap might casually throw a rock through the windshield of our car, but everyone we met – gas pump attendants, mainly – seemed too worn out and courteous to notice anything except the make of car we were driving.

We checked into a motel in Jackson and ate at a diner with neon in the windows where they served large portions of home-cooked food. After dinner we went back to the motel. I had forgotten to bring the condoms I had bought in New Orleans, but by the time that became evident we didn't care, or not enough anyway.

'If you've got AIDS I'll kill you,' Angela said, guiding me into her. 'And don't come inside me.'

After we had finished having sex – I came over her stomach, naturally – we lay in the almost darkness of Mississippi, car lights raking the ceiling, hearing the TV from the room next door.

'Have you ever been with a black girl before?'

'Yes.'

'How many?' she said, sounding relieved.

'Two. And you know the funny thing?'

'What?'

'They both asked me if I'd ever been with a black girl before.'

We had bought beer from a liquor store and spent the rest of the evening drinking in our room, like we had robbed a gas station and were on the run.

Back in New Orleans, Donelly and I also went on

excursions, out into the swamps – the things floating in the water like wood that had been drifting for thousands of years turned out to be alligators – or driving around the city, listening to rock tapes. One night we were driving on Filmore, just east of the City Park. It was raining slightly. The wipers smeared blurs of red across the windshield. Neon lay in green puddles. A car was waiting on lights up ahead and we drifted into it. We were not going fast but there was a loud noise of metal, a brief drizzle of glass. Two guys, black guys, got out and walked back towards us. Donelly had his hand on the glove compartment, which he opened. The guys checked out their beat-up station wagon, looking for damage. There was none, or at least there was no new damage, and they didn't seem too bothered. Donelly shut the glove compartment and wound down the window. One of the guys came over to talk with him. When he smelt the smell of grass in our car he started laughing and Donelly handed him the joint he had been smoking. Then the two black guys got back in their car and we two white guys went on our way. For a moment I had been extremely nervous. In America you are conscious of the race thing in a way that you never are in England. You find yourself in a black neighbourhood and you think, Shit, I'm in a black neighbourhood, maybe I shouldn't be here. Donelly said he'd been a little uneasy too, when they first got out of the car.

'That's why I carry this,' he said, opening the glove compartment and reaching inside. He passed me a gun. I had never held a gun before. It was small, heavy, black and dangerous looking. I handed it back to Donelly, who shut it up in the glove compartment again.

'Trouble is, I've only got two bullets left. It's like, what am I going to do if three guys try to fuck with me?'

I did not know what to say. I was from England and, as such, unfamiliar with the way of the gun.

'Two bullets,' said Donelly, shaking his head.

'Maybe you should buy some more bullets,' I said.

'You're right, dude. I've got to buy some more bullets.'

'Two bullets . . .'

'Shit, two bullets is like nothing.'

'What use is a gun with only two bullets?' I said. I was getting the hang of gun talk and really quite enjoying it.

'A gun needs six bullets,' said Donelly.

'As in six-shooter.'

'Basically I'm four bullets short.'

'You're working at thirty-three per cent of your potential capacity.'

'Six minus four equals two.'

'A shortfall of four.'

'A guy with only two bullets in his gun is a fucking pussy.'

'I didn't want to say it,' I said. 'I thought you might be offended.'

'Even though you didn't say it, I knew that's what you were thinking.'

'If I were you I'd go to the bullet shop tomorrow. First thing.'

'You know what I'm gonna do when I get there?'

'You're going to buy four bullets.'

'I might even buy six.'

'Good idea.'

'Then I'd have two spare.'

'Two spare, exactly.'

We parked the car outside our building and walked quickly – it was raining harder now – to the Port of Call. The Gulf War was over and the bar was rowdier than ever. We sat at the bar. Donelly had slept with the barmaid, the one I had tried to engage in conversation, and she let us have free drinks. I was hungry and ordered a burger; Donelly had already eaten dinner but he wanted one also. We'd been stoned before; now, with the drinking, we were getting fucked up. He told me about his time in the military. He had been stationed in Berlin, where he and a buddy had sold classified information to the Soviets on a regular basis. As a result they'd ended up with so much cash they were hard-pressed to spend it. They'd fly to Paris for the weekend, paying a thousand bucks a night for beautiful French hookers. He'd also started making headway with the coke habit which had gotten out of control in LA.

'Did you feel bad about it?'

'What? Blowing all that money on coke and whores?'

'No. Selling secrets to MI5 – I mean the KGB.'

'It just felt like easy money.'

'It sounds like treason to me.'

'Well it *was*, dude.'

Donelly was always telling me stuff like this, stuff about how untrustworthy he was – treasonously so – but it never occurred to me not to trust him, not to believe the stuff he told me. And not just that: in his way he seemed one of the most trustworthy people I had ever met, someone I could entrust things to – not that I had anything to entrust him with – without any fear of betrayal. All this means, I suppose, is that he was my friend. Living as I have, in many different cities, in different countries, I've got used to making new friends at an age when many people are living off the diminishing stockpile amassed at university, when they were nineteen or twenty. It's one of the things about the way I've lived that has made me happiest, and maybe the only reason I'm telling this story – this non-story – is to record the simple fact that in New Orleans, a town where we knew hardly anyone, Donelly and I became friends.

'You know, I'm still thinking about those bullets,' he said after we had finished our burgers and ordered more beer.

'I knew it,' I said. 'I could tell.'

'I could buy ten: four and six.'

'Two sets of six.'

'But I don't need that many.'

'So stick to six. I mean, *buy* six.'

'Two plus four.'

'Equals six.'

'Plus two left over.'

'Bingo!'

My time in New Orleans was drawing to an end. I was due in Santa Cruz, where I had arranged to sublet an apartment from a friend who was going travelling for a few months. Just as I was getting a life it was time to leave. As is often the case, the prospect of imminent departure manifested itself as an overwhelming urge to shop. At that stage of my life I did not wear sandals, but at Donelly's insistence I bought a pair of Tevas that fit my feet like a glove, like a glove on each foot – which means, I suppose, that they fit like socks. I also bought a pair of prescription sunglasses that made the world glow with a clarity and rosy-tinted brightness I had never seen before.

Donelly was thinking of going west too, but not too far west. If he ended up in LA again, he was sure he would kill himself. He was thinking of Las Vegas, which was 'west of New Orleans but not as far west as LA'.

'Right,' I said. 'Exactly.' He had friends there, in Vegas. From time to time we spoke of my collaborating with him on a book about his life. 'All the espionage shit' gave such a book considerable commercial potential, but I saw it as a kind of parable, one without any lesson or moral, a parable from which it would be impossible to learn anything or draw any conclusions. I was keen to do it and so was he.

Angela and I slept together a few more times after we got back from our freedom ride, but there was nothing happening really. We had seen each other so infrequently that the transition from seeing each other to not seeing each other was almost imperceptible. Perhaps I had begun to pick up some of Donelly's indifference to the way things turn out. That, I began to suspect, was not the only thing I had picked up. I was not feeling quite right: a slight burning, very slight, when I pissed.

The night before leaving, Donelly and I got stoned and sat by the Mississippi (allegedly an unwise thing to do after dark). The moon was almost full. Strictly speaking it was not a full moon, but it was full enough. I told Donelly about the freight I wished I'd hopped.

'You should have done it, dude,' he said.

'I know. I wrote about it instead.'

'That night I tried to kill myself, I almost didn't go ahead with it. I could hardly be bothered. Then I thought, What the fuck, you can sit here in your car drinking any night. Like c'mon, let's get on with it.'

'What willpower!'

Tankers went by, full of slow purpose, between us and the cranes of Algiers, across the water. There was no fog, but the sound of foghorns is a part of my memory of the scene. Every now and again the fullish moon was obscured by clouds making their way to the sea. The river did not seem like a strong brown god; it just seemed like a huge river, so old and heavy it had long ago lost all interest in making it to the Gulf of Mexico or wherever. Only the weight of implacable habit impelled it onwards.

The following morning Donelly drove me to the airport and I flew to San Francisco and took a bus to Santa Cruz. The burning sensation I felt when pissing had become unignorable. I went to a clinic, where I was given antibiotics for chlamydia.

Donelly and I spoke on the phone from time to time, but our plans to do a book together came to nothing: the novel I was writing took longer to complete than I had hoped – in fact I never completed it. Gradually we lost touch.

I heard from a friend recently that James and Ian had both died. The last I heard of Donelly, he was living in Las Vegas. When I tried to call him several years ago the number was unavailable. I had no fall-back address for him – this was in the days before e-mail – and have no idea where he is. I have moved many times since New Orleans and do not know if Donelly has tried to get in touch with me. From time to time I have thought about trying to track him down, but have no idea how to go about it. He could be in LA, he could be anywhere. Chances are, he has blown his brains out by now.

MISS CAMBODIA

At school, Circle was so long and skinny that the other kids called her Miss Cambodia, and then, when she was thirty-three, she went there – to Cambodia – with me. Seen in this light, our trip was a kind of homecoming, but although we were greeted warmly everywhere we went, no one realized that Circle was actually a former Miss Cambodia. To the Cambodians she was just another tall tourist, treated like royalty for the simple reason of the vastness of her wealth.

Before Circle became Circle she was called Sarah, but in the course of our travels in Southeast Asia names like Sarah and Jeff came to seem extremely boring. We kept meeting people called Vortex or Raven or Love Cat or – my favourite – Cloudy Bongwater, and so we decided that we too should adopt interesting names. But of course you cannot call yourself Circle until you have in some way *become* Circle, so although Sarah decided early on that she wanted to call herself Circle (after a little girl we had met in Goa and, in a surge of senti-ment, briefly considered adopting), she had to wait for the right moment to assume this identity. Having said that, we were also aware that assuming the name can hasten the develop-ment of the persona. It was the same dilemma as that faced

by writers seeking a name for their characters: it is no good
calling a character Dave if he is not a Dave, but equally, if
you refer to a character as X as a temporary expedient, it will
only impede his acquiring the characteristics appropriate to
his name, which might well turn out to be Brett or Sebastian
or Stan. Before she could become Circle, Sarah had to acquire
a kind of circularity of identity, an in-my-beginning-is-my-end
attitude to life, even, possibly, a stoner dippiness that was
quite out of character. Or so we thought. And then, in Ko
Pha-Ngan, a few nights before we flew to Cambodia, Sarah
simply introduced herself to someone as Circle without making
any other adjustment to her personality – and, oddly, it worked.
I was glad because although I was all in favour of her adopting
a new name, I liked Sarah the way she was and knew that
although I had been delighted by Love Cat, who informed us
of a fantastic deal on flights to Cambodia from Ko Samui, I
soon grew tired of her dippiness. Love Cat was wearing big
green bug-eye sunglasses when she told us about these cheap
air tickets.

'Where do you fly to in Cambodia?' asked Circle (who
at that stage was still called Sarah).

'Oh, I'm not sure,' said Love Cat. 'Saigon, I think.' It
was a splendid remark, but deep down, both of us knew that
even if she began calling herself Circle, Sarah would never
achieve that degree of geographical vagueness.

The flight was actually to Phnom Penh, a city about
which we knew almost nothing – except that it was not
Saigon. The streets had the desolate quality of towns in North
Africa, where there is nothing to do except grow old, an
impression enhanced by the fact that they were swarming

with young people whose lives were always going to fall short of their gifts for everything except survival and acquiescence. An energetic torpor held sway. Or maybe it was just the heat. There were no streetlights and the unlit streets were – as Dylan said of Rome – full of rubble. Cyclos drifted through this rubble like fish, like birds, like birds in an aquarium: like fish in their unruffled lack of urgency, like birds because they were perched high up on the saddles of their vehicles. These vehicles were not just how the cyclos earned their living, they were also where they lived. When they were not gliding around the city looking for customers or, more rarely, taking customers somewhere, they slept in their machines. (Does the word 'cyclo' refer to the carriage, or the man? Who can tell the dancer from the dance?) In an ideal world we would have bought a cyclo – the machine – shipped it to San Francisco, and taken it to Burning Man, where we could have offered people rides to any destination in Black Rock City. Presumably it was unbelievably hard work, being a cyclo, but since they only rarely got a fare and never went fast when they did, there was no sign of obvious effort as they pedalled through the debris-strewn streets. We had been warned that cyclos tend to keep going in a straight line, that if you wanted to avoid ending up in Thailand or Vietnam, you had to issue precise instructions about where you wanted to go. Apart from the fact that anywhere you wanted to go was always and inevitably 'very far', they appeared to have no knowledge of the layout of their city and little sense of direction (though as we grew more familiar with Cambodia this came to seem a quality common to much of the population rather than unique to cyclos). Several times we ended up where we had started without arriving at our destination, and it seemed, in the amazing heat, as if we had somehow circumnavigated the globe in thirty minutes.

These purposeless cyclo journeys often began and ended at the Foreign Correspondents' Club. It quickly became apparent that the distinguishing feature of this place was an absolute lack of foreign correspondents. There was as much chance of seeing Ryszard Kapuściński or James Fenton or John Pilger as there was of running into Bruce Willis in Planet Hollywood. It was a theme café that gave businessmen, tourists and engineers the chance to act like hard-drinking foreign correspondents without the irritating chore of having to file copy. That was fine by us. A breeze drifted in from the river and we liked sitting there, recovering from the debilitating heat and eating excellent pizzas from the wood-burning oven. When we were not in the Foreign Correspondents' Club we strolled around in the debilitating heat, which was really quite stultifying – so stultifying, in fact, that we stopped off at a barber's, where I had a haircut even though my hair didn't really need cutting. Some men are fussy about always going to the same barber – or hairdresser, rather – but I like having my hair cut by cheap barbers all over the world. It is a good, honest trade, barbering, and as long as you do not stray into the realm of over-priced salons and peroxide stylists, it is pretty consistent the world over. This barber had only one leg and spoke no English, but his ability to cut my hair – which he did skilfully, with considerable pride – was in no way compromised by either lack. A small crowd gathered to watch and grin as he snipped and buzzed his way around my head. When he had finished cutting my hair he massaged my head, neck and shoulders for good measure, and everybody involved in this transaction – including Circle and the other people watching – went away pleased.

After that we continued strolling the streets and seeing the sites, even though nothing in Phnom Penh was quite worth seeing. The Royal Pagoda, the Silver Pagoda, Wat Phnom . . . they were, as Circle put it in a postcard to her mum, 'nothing to write home about'. Taxi drivers urged us to go to the killing fields, but we were too hot and tired – the heat meant we were tired all the time – and had no desire to see piles of skulls, and so, whenever possible, we retired to the breezy familiarity of the Foreign Correspondents' Club.

Sitting there one evening we got talking to a sweating Texan who said, 'The only way to do a road trip in this goddam country is to go by boat.'

'You can always fly,' said Circle cheerfully. The Texan looked at her as if she were quite stupid, but since travelling by road – or more accurately, by lack of road – was so gruelling, we took his advice and bought tickets for the speedboat to Siem Reap. There were two boats, both full by the time we got to the dock – half an hour early, at six-thirty in the morning – but in Southeast Asia no form of transport is ever completely full, of course, and so we squeezed on to the roof with the other Westerners while the Cambodians stayed below, in the shade. The reddish brown banks of the Tonlé Sap River looked like small cliffs, evidence of how low the water level was at this late stage – rains were due any day – of the dry season. We set off exactly on time – and broke down almost immediately. After a short delay, we were off again, but this early mechanical problem did not, said Circle, 'bode well'.

It began to get very hot, but we were actually going pretty fast and the speed-generated breeze was cooling. The two boats travelled in tandem, taking it in turns to lead, bumping across each other's wakes. Sitting next to us was a Canadian with a Hemingway beard who explained that for half the year the river flowed in one direction and then, for the rest of the year, it flowed in the other. Rivers like to meander – it's in their nature – but this was the first time I had heard of one going into auto reverse.

'What a strangely consistent country it is,' said Circle. 'Even the river lacks a clear sense of direction.'

For a while we looked at the banks of this wide river even though there wasn't much to look at – a few huts, women washing clothes, kids waving and splashing, a bit of low-intensity squalor – and then I stopped paying attention to anything until I noticed that there was nothing to pay attention to: at some point the banks of the river had disappeared and we were surrounded by a flat expanse of nothing but water in every direction. The Tonlé Sap River had become the Tonlé Sap Lake.

Indifferent to this subtle but significant change, the boat powered on through the featureless lake. Although it was difficult to tell how fast we were going, it seemed like we were making excellent progress. I shaded my head with a sarong, was not even aware that I had fallen asleep until I was jolted awake by the boat abruptly slowing down. The propellers were throwing up gouts of thick black mud. We came to a standstill. The silence was sudden but the sudden increase in heat now that we were stationary was even more sudden. The captain jumped overboard and I was surprised to see him walk through water that came up only to his shins. Our sister ship had also stopped, some way ahead, whether in solidarity or because it too had run aground was impossible to say. The sun began beating down on us with a vengeance. It was utterly silent. There was no wind. The captain had walked off quite a way, trying, presumably, to find a channel of deeper water. The crew succeeded in lifting the propellers out of the mud; the motors, apparently, were not damaged. Two little fishing boats came up to try to tug us free, but the effort almost capsized them. Some Germans from our boat got out to push, but there were only four of them and these few hands made heavy work of it. Understandably they urged other passengers to join in, but I was nervous about bilharzia – which may or may not have been present in Cambodia – and didn't want to get my feet in the silver-brown water. A former Miss Cambodia, Circle naturally made no attempt to help. She preferred to languish in the scalding sun, contributing nothing to the self-rescue effort, rubbing high-factor sunscreen into her long legs and thin arms. Her hair streamed over her shoulders, glinting black and lovely, as if she had just stepped out of a shower.

Another boat came by and we tried combining our propellers with their tugging power, but still we did not budge. The situation grew increasingly desperate, especially when we noticed that our sister ship had vanished, leaving us – as Circle put it – 'as idle as a painted ship on a painted ocean'.

'Water, water everywhere,' I said.

'And not a drop to drink,' said Circle.

'Water, water everywhere . . .'

'And still the boards did shrink.'

Elsewhere on the boat, conversation among the tourists

began to turn on the incompetence of the captain. Since he did this trip every day, it was incredible that he had made such a stupid mistake – and it was even more stupid, once we hit the bottom, to have tried to plough on through the mud, the sole effect of which was to entrench the boat in it more deeply. Some way off to our left, spindly sticks stuck out from the surface of the lake, indicating a path from which we had veered. Why had the captain done that? Why had he deviated from the right way? These were the unanswered questions that tormented us as we sat on the baking roof. Our mood was both mutinous and impotent. Our Canadian friend who knew something about life on the Asian wave – he had been on three boats in the past fortnight, he said, and they had all broken down or run aground – insisted that the only way out of this fix was to unload everybody and everything from the boat in the hope that this would give it enough buoyancy to be tugged clear of the mud. No one acted on his advice. It was midday. The last of our drinking water was long gone. We had stopped sweating. The sun did what it did best: it pounded down on the lake and the boat and us. The sun was so strong that it seemed likely that the lake might come to the boil; that enough water would evaporate to lower the level of the lake and leave the boat more firmly stuck than ever.

'In a couple of hours,' I said to Circle, 'this boat is going to look like the raft of the *Medusa*.' The sun was beating down, taking a terrible toll. It was like being in a desert of water, a watery desert where there was nothing to be seen from horizon to horizon except the little fishing boats that rocked up with surprising regularity, all willing to lend a hand, none able to make any difference.

Eventually, exactly as advised by the Canadian, everybody on our boat was ferried across to one of these other boats. Under the infernal sun this precarious operation took for ever. In turn, the boat to which we had transferred became so heavily laden that it was on the brink of sinking – into about four inches of water. Still another boat lashed itself to our boat – the so-called speedboat, the boat we had recently abandoned – and from our new boat we watched as the combined effect of the propellers of our old boat, the engines of the boat tugging, and the sunburned Germans Fitzcarraldoing succeeded in moving it, our old boat, first an inch and then several feet. After that it was plain sailing. Free of the mud, the boat roared with all its unleashed power, and someone – me, actually – initiated a round of applause and cheers in gratitude to 'the lovely people of Cambodia' for coming to our rescue.

Heads throbbing from the heat, we were all ferried back to our old boat, ready to continue a trip which had gone from being an adventure to an ordeal that was far from over. We were on the move again but we were, so to speak, not out of the woods yet. Already severely compromised, our faith in the captain soon sank to a new low. If we were making progress there was no sign that this was the case. Nothing had changed. The Tonlé Sap Lake extended in every direction. There was no sign of land.

'You know what?' said Circle.

'What?' I said.

'I think we're going round in circles.'

'You think what, Circle?'

'I said, "I think we're going round in circles."'

'You just said that,' I said. 'We're going round in circles.'

'Seriously. I think we are.'

And so we were. Dazed by the sun, it took a while to sink in, but eventually I had to concede that Circle was right: we were indeed going round and round, in wider and wider circles. Why? Had the poor sense of direction we had noticed in the cyclos of Phnom Penh – and in the River Tonlé Sap itself – taken hold of our captain as well? There were no landmarks, just the endless expanse of lake, but the boat was surely equipped with a compass. The sun was pounding down. My head throbbed. The lake was undisturbed by any movement other than the dissolving coil of our wake. Gradually the knowledge of what was happening spread like despair among the other passengers, one of whom tapped me on the shoulder and, in a hoarse whisper, said, 'We're going round in circles.' I nodded and tapped Circle on the shoulder.

'We're going round in circles,' I said.

Eventually the other boat – our companion vessel and sister ship – came back and led us to Siem Reap, which we left five days later. The prospect of returning to Phnom Penh by boat was too awful to contemplate and so we decided to head to Battambang, allegedly 'an elegant riverside town rich in colonial ambience'. We were under the impression that a taxi was taking us from the Mahogany guesthouse to the boat, but the taxi turned out to be a pickup, and by the time it had finished making all its pickups, twelve of us were crammed into the back and four in the front with the driver. As we headed out of Siem Reap the road did what all roads in Cambodia do: it deteriorated. The sun came up, boiling, undeterred, right on time. The pickup lurched and bucked over the ruts and holes and craters of the road that was barely a road.

'Is this a 4-WD, as they say? Even though that actually has more syllables than "four-wheel drive",' said Circle. I didn't know, but thought her point about the syllables was well made. Coming towards us, a boy on a bike wavered, wobbled and finally lost control, spilling his cargo into the dust: two huge baskets of little silver-grey fish. Without anger or complaint he began picking them up, shovelling them back into his bamboo panniers. Ahead of us was a motorbike with a big sealed basket – the size of two heavy rucksacks – on the back. Every time the motorbike went over a bump this basket emitted piggy squeals of unconditional terror. As we drew close we saw why: the basket was crammed with about a dozen piglets. Their conditions were so abject, their treatment so deplorable, their squealing so hysterical, it was hard to imagine any form of life having a worse time at that particular moment anywhere on earth. Their plight was a final proof of – and simultaneously a reproof to – the arguments of animal rights activists. I had never seen animals treated so abysmally, but in a country whose people had endured the very worst that history could throw at them, who gave a toss about piglets? Especially once our destination became apparent: the Vietnamese floating village. We clambered out of the pickup and transferred to some little boats that ferried us to the makeshift quays – floating, like everything else – from which we would head to our various destinations: Battambang, Phnom Penh or wherever.

All visitors to the developing world, if they are honest, will confess that they are actually quite keen on seeing a bit of squalor: people living on garbage dumps, shanty towns, that kind of thing. In India we met a Swede who had strayed into one of the worst slum districts of Bombay. To elicit his sympathy and money a woman who was begging shoved her dead baby in his face. There was a group of about six of us listening to this story; we were all horrified and, I think, more than a little envious. The Vietnamese floating village may not have been as bad as that but it was seriously squalid: a collection of dilapidated huts with almost nothing in them, floating in a brown soup of water. It didn't even look like it was floating: it looked like it was *sinking*. There was litter – plastic bottles, paper, cans, vegetable waste – bobbing about everywhere. The water was filthy but little patches of slime and ooze had coagulated to form conurbations of super-concentrated filth. I kept my mouth tightly closed in case a drop of water from this vast floating cesspool entered my lips. Meanwhile the residents – smiling, happy, waving – decorated their verandas with blazing red geraniums and bathed their children and washed their clothes in this fetid liquid. If any passengers from the pickup were obliged to stay here, they – we – would have been dead in a month, possibly in a week.

We moored next to a hut that served as the terminal for boats to and from Battambang. The boats did not look like the ones pictured on the tickets we had bought the day before; in fact they did not look like working boats at all. They looked like the husks of boats that had been plundered for spares, stripped of everything that worked. But yes, these were our boats and we boarded them in numbers far exceeding all standards of maritime safety. When the boats were full, a couple more people were crammed on to each one and their rucksacks piled into what little space remained. Then we sat and waited. We waited for so long that I began to need a piss. I wasn't sure what to do: piss off the side of the boat? Would people mind? Wouldn't that be like pissing in someone's garden? Or their lounge? We waited and waited. The pressure in my bladder increased. I didn't know what to do. Then I did. Bobbing in the water, less than a foot from our boat, was a massive human turd. It looked like a huge corn shuck. I did not want to see it but I could not take my eyes off it. Indeed, in an environment conducive only to diarrhoea and cholera, its firmness and size were a colossal achievement – a testament to man's ability to adapt to his environment. It was a monstrous thing but it solved the question of where I could piss. I stood on the edge of the boat and, in full view of everyone, taking care not to lose my balance, played my part in making a foul place more pestilential still.

That is how we arrived in and departed from Siem Reap, but what of Angkor? What about the wonders of Preah Kahn, Bayon and Ta Prohm? I'd show you my snaps but unfortunately there aren't any. I don't even own a camera. Circle has one and she did take a few pictures, but to be quite honest, they're not worth the Kodak paper they're printed on. Circle knows a lot about lots of things; she can play the piano and the violin; but she knows nothing about photography, not even the basics, not even the stuff I know. She shoots into the sun, stands in the light when shooting into shadow. Her line on this is simple.

'If I see something I like, I photograph it.'

'Irrespective of light, of where the sun is?'

'Yes.'

'Or how far away the thing you want to photograph is?'

'Yes.'

'Hence those recurring motifs in your work: the murky silhouette, the picture that to all intents and purposes has nothing in it . . .'

Despite this demoralizing sarcasm Circle did take a few pictures at Angkor, mainly of me: blurred beneath the roots of trees dripping like candle wax over the walls of Ta Prohm, blinking next to the stone faces of Bayon, over-exposed as an albino at Preah Kahn. None of them is worth a second glance, most are not worth a first. With some justification Circle blamed this on my bad attitude. Whenever I saw her produce her camera I would always say something like, 'Here comes Eve Arnold on assignment,' or, 'Ah, I see the indecisive moment is once again upon us.' Such moments were actually few and far between; Circle may have taken more pictures than I, but compared with our fellow tourists she was, as I quipped, 'well below Parr'. In the eyes of these visitor-photographers this made us second-class citizens. People taking photographs had unquestionable priority at all the best spots. You scarcely had the right to be at some iconic locations unless you were taking photographs. We were the lowest possible caste of tourists: the unseeables. As such we often had to wait for whole tour groups to have their pictures taken before we could walk, sit or even look. At some level, because we weren't taking photographs at Angkor, we weren't actually there.

But we were there even if we don't have the photographs

– or only half a dozen – to prove it. We spent the first day making the rounds, exactly as advised by the guidebook. We saw Bayon at dawn, went on to some other places, headed back to Siem Reap for a nap, returned to Angkor in the afternoon and to Phnom Bakheng, the hill overlooking Angkor Wat, for the sunset.

Sunsets impose a heavy burden on the sightseer. A spot acquires such a reputation as the place from which 'to watch the sunset' that you are virtually obliged to go there. Phnom Bakheng was just such a spot. It was a punishing walk, hauling ourselves up the slope, but my Tevas, the Tevas I had bought years earlier in New Orleans, were able to take the strain. As we walked up that punishing hill I thought of writing to Teva and suggesting a couple of slogans: 'Tevas Can Take It' was one. Perhaps there was only one.

When we finally got to the top it was rammed, like a party waiting to kick off. We expected to see a DJ, decks, banks of speakers. There were hundreds, possibly thousands of people, but they weren't waiting for a party – they were waiting for the sunset. The Japanese were out in force. Everyone – us included – was spraying or smearing themselves with insect repellent because the mosquitoes were also out in force. Serious photographers had their cameras on tripods. One such photographer turned to his wife and said, 'Fifteen minutes to go,' as though they were colleagues at Mission Control at NASA. Everyone else simply waited. For the sunset. Except for a few all-important details, the scene was reminiscent of Hampi, in India, where we had also flocked to watch the sunset. Pessoa was right: there's no point going to Constantinople to see a sunset; they're the same the world over. But you do it anyway; you go to Constantinople and Phnom Bakheng and everywhere else, and while you're there you catch the sunset. While travelling, in fact, watching the sunset gives the day a purpose and meaning it can otherwise lack. Even so, few things seem more idiotic than waiting on a sunset. Waiting for the sunset becomes an activity, an exercise in abeyance. Idleness, doing nothing, is raised to the level of sharply focused purpose. Expectation becomes a form of sustained exertion. You wait for it to happen even though it's going to happen anyway. Or not happen. Frank O'Hara was right: 'The sun doesn't necessarily set, sometimes it just disappears.' And when it does deign to set? Auden got that right:

> Goethe put it neatly:
> No one cares to watch the
> Loveliest sunset after
> Quarter of an hour.

It would be OK if there were something else to do, if you weren't just looking at the sunset. *I* got that right.

'Driving into the sunset might be bad for your eyes,' I said to Circle as we waited for the sunset. 'But at least you're not just looking at it, at least you're *driving*. That's how I like my sunsets. I like local ones too, the ones over Acre Lane and Lambeth Town Hall in November, the ones I look at quickly when all I can think about is getting home in time – though normally I'm there already, watching the end of *Neighbours*, waiting for the six o'clock news.'

We may have taken a dim view of waiting for the sunset, but that's what we did every night in Angkor: we waited for the sunset. By our fourth day, as well as the sunsets and the sunrises, we had seen everything we wanted to see, except Pre Rup, a temple some way off to the east of Angkor Wat. We had seen most things twice, but the only time we had been to Pre Rup was when we zoomed past it, by accident, on the backs of two motorbike taxis which had got lost on their way from Bayon to Ta Prohm (like a London taxi getting lost on the way to Big Ben from Buckingham Palace). For one panicky moment I even thought they were trying to abduct us – but no, in the friendly Cambodian way, they had simply got lost.

We returned there, to Pre Rup, on our last day, the day before we were taking the boat to Battambang. In the course of the previous three days we'd seen so many temples I would be hard-pressed to say what the distinguishing features of this one were apart from the fact that it was near another, almost identical one. We were templed out. Our minds had been blown. Repeatedly. Angkor had swallowed us up, devoured us just as the jungle had consumed Ta Prohm. The experience had been too huge and, because of the millions of carvings – most of which I scarcely noticed – too intensely intricate. We were suffering from stupendousness-overload and, as usual, it was about a thousand degrees centigrade and humid as an old pond.

Before we had even begun to climb the first steps of Pre Rup, children came running up, wanting us to buy Coke from them. A girl with a wide face and a question-mark-shaped scar above her eyebrow was faster than the rest. It so happens that I did want a Coke. As anyone who has travelled in Southeast Asia will tell you, these occasions – when you actually want something someone is hawking – are to be treasured. Ninety-nine times out of a hundred what is offered is not wanted, either because it is utterly useless, or because although it is utterly useless you have six of it already (because you felt obliged, on some previous occasion, to buy something you did not want). But yes, there are those rare occasions when people are selling something you really want. It is a joyous moment for all concerned. On this occasion she was selling a Coke and I wanted a Coke. More precisely, I wanted *half* a Coke because Coke always grows disgusting after four gulps, however much you enjoy those four gulps. Circle feels the same about Coke; sometimes two gulps are enough for her; and so, on our behalf, I accepted a can from the girl who had been first to offer one to us.

My hands had just taken possession of the can when another prospective vendor came up. He was a boy of about twelve, on crutches, with one leg amputated below the knee. This was his bad leg, or so we thought. Then we saw that his other leg – the good leg – was actually a wooden leg; it was, in other words, a very bad leg indeed; in fact, it was not a leg at all. We had seen plenty of legless children in the course of our time in Cambodia, but this boy touched us to the quick: it was as if the ruined, resilient spirit of Cambodia had suddenly appeared before us. He had a lovely smile. In a country of lovely smiles, where the ability to keep smiling had been more ruthlessly tested than anywhere on earth, where a smile was both a denial of history and a victory over it, his was an amazing smile. He had light brown skin and thin arms and dark hair. He was wearing a blue T-shirt, faded, perfect in the way that T-shirts always are on young boys and girls, that is to say they look great whatever is printed on them (in this case the Nike logo).

I changed my mind. I put the girl's Coke back in the gleaming ice of her plastic bucket and bought one from this boy. I took my custom elsewhere, shifted my allegiances, betrayed the girl totally. The boy walked with us while we drank our Coke, followed by the girl, who was now holding the Coke I had placed back in her bucket. He was smiling but she was not. She took this poaching of her custom very badly. She kept asking us to buy a Coke from her, but by now we were sitting down, well into our shared Coke, and the thought of another one was not pleasing to us. She began cursing us in Cambodian. We did not understand what she was saying but we did not need to know what she was saying to know that it was abusive. It was the first time we had glimpsed anything resembling what used to be called Asiatic cruelty, and even this amounted to no more than abusing a cheapskate tourist for not buying her Coke. Then, abruptly, she changed tack and began snivelling. She even squeezed out a few tears. When this made *us* smile she reverted to abusing us. We asked the boy to translate.

'She wants you to buy her Coke,' he said.

'Is that all she's saying?'

'Yes, she would like you to buy her Coke. She very angry that you buy Coke from me, that you don't buy her Coke.'

'You buy my Coke,' she said in English.

I shook my head.

The Coke in question was standing in the sun, getting hot, becoming less and less appetising by the minute.

'You buy Coke from me.'

I shook my head.

'You buy my Coke,' she yelled.

I shook my head. At some level we were engaged in a colossal battle of wills, and my will had hardened horribly. The iron had entered my soul. I would not be budged.

'You buy one Coke from me.'

I shook my head.

She made another attempt at snivelling. I laughed and once again she reverted to abuse. Meanwhile, with all the resignation and acceptance of someone who has lived to a hundred, the boy from whom we had bought our Coke was telling us how he had lost his legs. He had gone to fetch a cow that had fallen asleep in a field and he had stepped on a land mine. It was a typical story; we had heard variants of the same story dozens of times before in Cambodia, but they had never affected us so powerfully. There was some confusion, however, about when exactly this accident had happened.

'Seven years ago,' he said.

'How old were you when you lost your legs?'

'Ten.'

'How long ago was that?'

'Seven years.' It didn't make sense. We couldn't work out whether he had lost his legs aged ten or seven. We asked again but the figures did not change. He lost his legs when he was ten, seven years ago.

'So how old are you now?' asked Circle. He could have been ten, was probably twelve, thirteen at most.

'Seventeen,' he said. He was a lovely boy who looked about twelve but was seventeen. He had lost both legs and we had bought a Coke from him instead of buying one from the girl who continued, intermittently, to abuse us. At one point she picked up the can of Coke as though she were going to throw it at us, or even club us with it. Instead she thumped it down on the ground.

'You buy Coke from me!' she insisted, but by this point her drink had become frankly unsellable: it was boiling hot and highly explosive. Whoever opened it would be sprayed with hot Coke and in seconds this sweet liquid would attract an army of ants and insects. In any case we had by now hardened our hearts against her. We had it in our power to resolve the situation by buying a Coke from her but we didn't want to buy a Coke from her. Our power was absolute and we were implacable. We were touched by the boy who stood for the plight of his country but we were not going to alleviate the distress of this girl who was, by turns, weeping and abusive. If the boy seemed to us the incarnation of Cambodia, to her we were the incarnation of all the fickle power and wealth of the West. She wanted us to buy a Coke – not a coconut, not something that grew here, but a Coke, manufactured under licence from the United States – and we would not buy a Coke from her. It was as simple as that. The injustice of it was almost perfect.

She had now reverted to snivelling, but both snivelling and abuse were equally ineffective against us. Even her persistence was to no avail. Not for the first time in my life I experienced a strange buckling, or warping, of time. I was actually wishing that I had bought a Coke from her, but it was already too late to do anything about it even though there was still time to do so. If there is anything to the idea of karma and reincarnation, then I will be reborn not as the legless boy from whom we bought a can of Coke but as the snivelling, angry girl from whom we did not buy one. Or maybe I will be reborn as the can of Coke itself: thumped on the ground, hot and unwanted, primed to explode. Most likely, though, the circle will be unbroken and I will – as Nietzsche maintained – be reborn as myself and will repeat this same scene, this same mistake and all the others that led to it, endlessly, throughout all eternity.

We got up to leave.

As we descended the temple steps I could hear the boy from whom we had bought our Coke calling to us, saying goodbye.

'Thank you, sir,' he was saying. 'Good luck in your life, sir. Have a good life, sir.' I looked back. He was balanced on his crutches, the stump of one leg hanging in mid-air, silhouetted against the tremendous sun, waving goodbye.

THE INFINITE EDGE

Oh Ubud, lovely, boring Ubud! It was so lovely, but we were there too long, far too long, and became somewhat demoralized by all the time we had on our hands. Much of that time was squandered at Munut Bungalows, just west of the centre of town, where I thrashed each of the staff at Ping-Pong. For most of the day the staff – eight teenage boys – moped about, doing nothing; at night they crowded round the TV watching things get blown up. If I strode into the reception area and made the sign for Ping-Pong – big grin, mimed backhand and forehand swipes of the hand – they leapt into action, wheeled out the table, and took it in turns to be thrashed by their favourite guest, who (aside from his girlfriend) was also their only guest. Yes, I beat them all. Except Madi, the manager. He and I faced each other in what was effectively the final of the Munut Open. It was touch and go but I lost because I wanted to win so badly that I was destined to lose. I alternated between overcautious defensive play and surges of all-out aggression. My trusty (in the sense of wildly untrustworthy) forehand smash let me down because I can only relax into that kind of attacking game when I am slightly ahead, when I'm confident, when I have the cushion of a five- or six-point advantage,

47

but on this occasion I got off to a bad start, fell slightly behind, and found that I was at a five- or six-point disadvantage, on the wrong side of the cushion, so to speak. I lost that game, and from then on, even when – by pure assertion of will – I managed to even things up at 2–2, I knew I was destined to lose, because I wanted to win too badly. Circle was watching and this made me want to win even more badly, and the more badly I wanted to win, the closer I brought myself to eventual defeat. Things began to go wrong in the early stages of the first game when I unleashed my forehand prematurely, thereby putting myself under immediate and unnecessary pressure. I achieved occasional spectacular successes but too often I smacked the ball into the net or beyond the edge of the table, and gradually the gap between us increased and I had to resort to simply getting the ball back safely, hoping Madi would make a mistake – which he rarely did because by that time he was feeling confident enough to punish my increasing timidity by smashing the ball back more or less at will.

These Ping-Pong games lent a sense of purpose to our stay in Ubud that it would otherwise have lacked. Charming though it is, the town is thoroughly overrun by tourism, even though there was actually a dearth of tourists when we were there. Political instability elsewhere in Indonesia meant that even at this, the peak time of the year, most hotels were so desperate for custom that it was possible to negotiate such heavy discounts on rooms that it amounted to a form of economic sanction. Ubud already had the highest concentration of boutique hotels in the world, and yet, even though most of the boutique hotels were almost empty, more boutique hotels were being built. ('And *still* they build!' said Circle in astonishment and admiration.) You could not move for boutique hotels and people selling sarongs and offering 'transport'. Every time we went out there were dozens of people offering accommodation, sarongs and 'transport'. It was a buyer's market and no one was buying anything. Some tourists became irritated by the unavoidable offer of 'Transport?' but the pervasiveness of the question – and the low level of expectation that accompanied it – led us to regard it in a new light. Saying 'Transport?', raising two fists to chest height, and moving them up and down slightly as though gripping an invisible steering wheel, was, we decided, the Balinese equivalent of waving and saying, 'Hi, how ya doin'?': a greeting in the form of an offer.

We rarely needed transport, preferring as we did to take walks in the rice paddies near the various boutique hotels, guesthouses, and *losmen* we stayed in during the course of the long weeks we squandered in beautiful, boring Ubud.

We'd never seen anything as green as these rice paddies. It was not just the paddies themselves: the surrounding vegetation – foliage so dense the trees lost track of whose leaves were whose – was a rainbow coalition of one colour: green. There was an infinity of greens, rendered all the greener by splashes of red hibiscus and the herons floating past, so white and big it seemed as if sheets hung out to dry had suddenly taken wing. All other colours – even purple and black – were shades of green. Light and shade were degrees of green. Greenness, here, was less a colour than a colonising impulse. Everything was either already green – like a snake, bright as a blade of grass, sidling across the footpath – or in the process of becoming so. Statues of the Buddha were mossy, furred with green. Stone had become plant, the inanimate had become organic. 'Annihilating all that's made / To a green thought in a green shade'? No, even thought had been annihilated. This was an entirely sensual green, one that rendered thought not just impossible but inconceivable.

However green the accompanying vegetation, the brightest green of all was still found in the rice paddy. To become truly itself the rice had to be surrounded by the deepest, lushest greens, thereby obliging the paddy to achieve that extra degree of greenness of which only it was capable. There could be only one winner. Relatively speaking only the rice paddy was really green. Only the rice paddy *hummed* with green.

So it was the green we noticed: that and the amazing fertility of everything, how willing and eager everything was just to grow, to grow for all it was worth, for the sheer fun of growing.

'The tree's being consists entirely in growing,' said Circle in the course of one of our walks.

'I disagree.'

'So do I.'

'Waving its leaves in the wind. Providing a perch for birds, being something the sky can enclose. Being something to be climbed. These are all parts of the tree's being.'

'But something else too, I think.'

'Being seen. Doing its bit for tourism.' I looked at Circle. I thought I had had the last word. Then I realized she had kept something up her sleeve – but I was not expecting that something to be in French.

'"*Arbre*,"' she said, '"*toujours au milieu de tout ce qui l'entoure . . .*" Guess who?'

'I'm torn between Baudelaire and Jonny 'Alliday.'

'Very funny.'

'But I'm going to plump for Rilke,' I said, pleased to catch the look of crestfallen admiration that passed over her face.

We were walking through rice paddies as we were having this conversation, trying to outdo each other and help each other along. The landscape was so fertile it looked wild, but it wasn't wild at all – it was actually entirely cultivated. The trees growing haphazardly on the fringes of the fields all played their part in the vegetative economy. Nothing was entirely decorative, but the extravagant scale of decoration – leaves the size of trees – obscured this from our view. There was an inevitability about the landscape. It was so harmonious as to seem to have cultivated itself. The rice terraces were stacked in geometric contours so that the scenery appeared all the time to be mapping itself.

'In their early stages the green shoots of rice grow in a mirror of themselves,' I said. 'Effectively, they're growing in a carefully tended patch of sky.'

'Sorry, I wasn't listening.'

'I said, "The constant surfacing or landing of insects means that the waterlogged rice paddy always looks as if it is being pockmarked by rain. Even on a clear day. This creates the impression that there is a huge delay in the mirror's capacity for reflection; either that or – and it amounts to the same thing – a corresponding gift for prophecy. Ultimately the mirror disappears but by then the rice—"'

'Having absorbed the sky-reflecting water—'

'"Has become an ideal representation of itself." Exactly.'

'That isn't what you said at all,' said Circle.

It was difficult walking through the rice paddy without a guide. We were unsure of the point at which strolling turned to trespass, appreciation to invasion. Because we were walking, I thought to myself later, when we were back at the Padma Indah (where we stayed after we had moved from Munut Bungalows), we didn't see much because we had to concentrate on where we were putting our feet.

'Still,' said Circle (who in the course of an earlier walk had slipped into a drainage ditch and sprained her ankle slightly), 'better walking in them than *working* in them.'

'Yes,' I said. 'Best just to look, to enjoy the view.'

We'd seen plenty of views like this elsewhere in Bali and Lombok. The most basic cottage (not that there was anything basic about our room at Waka di Ume, where we stayed for one night prior to moving into Munut Bungalows: Circle had cunningly got us upgraded from a basic to a luxury villa) was redeemed and elevated by the view. Anyone with a room to rent knew what tourists wanted: a 'view'. We investigated all sorts of places to stay before we decided on one extravagant night at Waka di Ume, before moving into that temple of Ping-Pong, the Munut. As they threw back the shutters to unleash a blaze of green, the owners would smile and say, 'Nice view,' but it always felt like an imported notion, something they had become familiar with through contact with tourists. It was, Circle said, as if they knew the word but did not share the mental space that enabled us – Circle and me and the other tourists, most of whom had stayed away in droves – to think in terms of 'the view'.

'Otherwise,' she continued, 'how could they litter so

indiscriminately? Littering and enjoyment of the view are fundamentally incompatible.'

'When you know something intimately you are often, simultaneously, oblivious to it,' I said. We were sitting down now, enjoying the view, not oblivious to it at all. A few yards ahead of us was a spindly, wind-driven bird scarer. We decided we would recreate it as a primitivist sculpture in the desert, at Black Rock City, but Circle did not have her camera with her and although I had my notebook, I did not have a pen or pencil, and so we had to try to commit its construction to memory. It consisted of . . . Unfortunately we could not remember how it was made, and so, needless to say, we did not make it – or anything like it – at Black Rock City. Having finished our examination of the bird scarer, we were free to reflect, more generally, on what we had learned in the course of our walk.

'The view, strictly speaking, is the product of a separation of leisure and labour,' I said. I had no idea if what I was saying was accurate – I was making it up as I went along – but I carried on regardless. 'Not surprisingly, then, this view is improved by – in fact, almost demands – the sight of people toiling in its midst, actively engaged in its creation and preservation. It's like that bit in *Jean de Florette* or *Manon des Sources* when Gérard Depardieu asks a peasant if he likes the view. The peasant doesn't know what he's talking about. You have to be a stranger to the landscape to regard it as a view. This idea of the view – or prospect – was once the preserve of a small ruling elite, then it became a bourgeois right; now that travel has been democratized, the view is available for everyone – except the people who are employed to maintain it.'

'In keeping with this,' said Circle, 'the place from which you are enjoying the view often blights the view of the people whom you are viewing.'

We sat back and enjoyed the view. In a manner of speaking. It would be more accurate to say what I said to Circle after a few minutes of sitting and looking.

'I see the view,' I said. 'I view the view, but I can't participate in the act of seeing it.'

'That's the covenant of the rice paddy,' said Circle. 'Separation is the price you pay for not having to work in them.'

'I feel it in other kinds of landscape too,' I said. 'At the vista points of the Grand Canyon, for example.'

'Perhaps the separation is more fundamental,' said Circle. 'The alienation of urban man – or you at any rate – from the natural world.'

'It's only when I'm stoned,' I said, 'that I feel a part of the landscape, when I can see the landscape as a bird or tree might see it, that I can enjoy the view – and it is, of course, at that exact moment that the view is no longer a view.'

Various attempts have been made to dissolve this separation of viewer from the view. The best example is the overflow pool, which has become such a feature of upmarket resorts in Bali, like Sayan Terrace, where we stayed when we came back to Ubud after an abortive trip to Lovina with our friend Gregor from Munich, whom we had met at the Kuang Si waterfalls, near Luang Prabang, in Laos. Instead of staying a boring four or five inches below the edge of the pool, the water flows over the rim into a surrounding channel and from there is pumped back into the main pool. By jumping in the pool you displace more water and the flow over the edge increases. You float in the pool, the water falls away, and there is, it seems, nothing to separate you from the view of the gorge, the river valley, the rice paddies. Distance, space, is abolished.

As we sat in the overflow pool at Sayan Terrace what I was seeing reminded me of something I remembered – the waterfalls at Kuang Si – and when I remembered this I realized what should have been obvious all along: that the infinity-edge pool was a man-made, architectural equivalent of the effect often found in waterfalls, like the one in Kuang Si where we had met Gregor.

Seen from below, the water tumbled down the cliff at a ferocious, deafening rate, but you could sit quite safely at the lip of the falls while the water spilled gently over the edge with no risk of your being taken with it. We'd been to quite a few waterfalls before – wretched, pissy little things – and went to Kuang Si somewhat half-heartedly. The water poured into a turquoise pool. In the rocks behind the vertical water were slippery caves you could sit in, like a primitive form of life, looking out through the wall of water at highly evolved humans. One of these humans, a dreadlocked Israeli, climbed into one of the caves and simply disappeared. Through the crystal curtain of water we saw his Teva-clad feet scrabbling up the slippery rock of the side of the cave. We kept expecting him to reappear but he did not.

It was *quite* nice being at the waterfall: worth going to, but we wouldn't have rated it higher than that. Then we learned that there was another tier higher up, at the point from which the water pouring on to us was falling. We toiled up an Aquirre path to one side of the waterfall, in deep shadow flecked by gold light, scrambling upward, clinging to the roots of trees. En route we fell in with a shaven-headed Australian and Gregor (also shaven-headed), with whom we later became friends. It was a difficult climb but I was wearing my trusty Tevas, of course. My Tevas took the strain. I had been wearing them every day for months. I was at one with my Tevas.

The view from the top of the falls was like nothing I had ever seen. The sky was a high-altitude blue, the mountains were covered in an impenetrable moss of prehistoric jungle. All of this was visible from a pool – at the base of a still higher set of falls – which became the source of the falls below, the falls we had recently walked up from. It was impossible to judge distance: everything was right next to us and impossibly remote. Although I have not really read or understood Heidegger, I took Gregor's word for it when he said that we were experiencing something akin to his – Heidegger's – definition of thought: the 'coming-into-the-nearness of distance'. The landscape converged on this spot and extended endlessly from it. It was like the transparent eyeball of the world. We sat there in this vast overflow pool, looking out over the infinite edge. The landscape was huge and microscopic. We sat in the pool but we were not admiring the view; we were a part of everything we saw.

Our trip to the waterfall at Kuang Si does not make sense except in the context of a game of Ping-Pong that had taken place a few days earlier. It was only my second game in Luang Prabang and we had played for a long time, in my opponent's tropical garden. The air was so humid that I was drenched in sweat after a minute. Eventually I beat my opponent 21–19 in a seven-game clash of contrasting styles (English aggression versus Oriental cunning). I knew I had pulled a muscle in my back (possibly because my T-shirt was soaked in sweat) but kept playing anyway. The next day my back was so bad we went to see a blind masseur, who dug his fingers so deeply into my back I expected him to pluck a bloody tumour from its depths. If anything, this made my bad back even worse. By the time we hobbled up to the waterfall, every step jarred my back.

In the course of our relationship I had often told Circle that I loved to jump from great heights into deep water, and now, at the waterfall, I had the chance to jump, but I could not risk jumping because the shock of impact combined with the cold water would undoubtedly have sent my muscle into an even deeper spasm that could easily have resulted in a trapped nerve or a slipped disc.

Years earlier, in the Caribbean, some friends and I had travelled on a boat from Anguilla to Sombrero, a rock in the middle of the sea. There was nothing on this island-rock except bird shit and a lighthouse, and once every fortnight a boat arrived with supplies and a new shift – perhaps the right word is 'crew' or 'team' – of lighthouse workers. When we got to Sombrero we walked for half a mile to the other side of the island, where there was an inlet. The sea entered the inlet through a very narrow gap of about ten feet. Then it widened into a circle, a pool almost. You could jump off the cliff – the height of the top board in a municipal pool – into deep water. Then, if you swam out beyond the little gap in the rock, you were in deep blue. The waters were shark-infested, and although I was worried about sharks I was happy jumping off the rocks into the pool. At first we jumped cautiously, inching tentatively towards the edge. Then we began taking running leaps, in pairs, holding hands, waggling our legs and arms in the air, and whooping like cowboys at a rodeo. I liked jumping off the rock but I also liked snorkelling along beneath the surface and seeing people come crashing through the blue in a white surge of bubbles. A couple of times I swam out between the narrow gap in the rocks, into the fathomlessness. There was nothing but blue in every direction. It was lovely but you felt so utterly out of your depth that it was easy to become frightened. We were in the sea, there were sharks in the sea. As soon as I thought about sharks I swam in again, but then, because it was so beautiful, I swam out again. Then I swam back in and looked at the others all jumping off the rock and I climbed up and jumped off again myself.

In its way the jump at Kuang Si required more daring than the one at Sombrero because you had to jump out quite a long way to clear a protruding rock six feet below. The danger was real but slight, slight but real. If you hit that rock you would be in serious trouble, but it was relatively easy to clear that rock and land in the deep water of the pool that flowed over the infinite edge and formed the waterfall that crashed into the lower level pool from which we had recently ascended. The shaven-headed Australian and Gregor both did the jump but I didn't. Gregor did an even more daring jump from a Tarzan tree that grew precariously over the pool, but I didn't do that either, of course. I didn't jump at all: I slithered stiffly down to the pool. They were younger than me, Gregor and the shaven-headed Australian, twenty years younger, half my age, roughly the age, in fact, that I was when I spent the afternoon jumping into the blue water at Sombrero. Now, twenty years later, I didn't feel my age, I felt twice my age, like an old man. Virility of one kind or another is so important if you are to feel like a man. You have to be able to perform stunts. You have to be able to show off in front of your woman, do things she urges you not to do because they look dangerous. I love jumping, I love showing off, but I was unable to jump because I had pulled a muscle in my back playing Ping-Pong, which I love even more than jumping. I longed to jump but I could not jump, so Circle and I inched our way down the slippery rocks and sat in the freezing pool, engulfed by a landscape that made it possible to believe that even at this late stage the world was an unexplored wilderness, vast, unmappable, full of wonder: an Eden whose size alone ensured there was no possibility of expulsion.

From the infinite edge we could see people in the pools below, lying on rocks, swimming, many of whom had no inkling of what was up here. One who did was the dreadlocked Israeli last seen clambering into a cave down there. He re-emerged from some rocks to our left, having dragged himself up to this higher tier of existence by his own sandal straps. It was like being a god up there. Except that we knew that other people had ascended to the next level of the falls and were, in all probability, looking down on us from another, higher infinite edge. This led, in turn, to an irresistible conclusion about the gods of Mount Olympus, namely that they had *their* gods too. For all their massed omniscience and omnipotence they almost certainly felt that over Olympus there towered a level of super-elevation from which their comings and goings were observed with humorous and sadistic indifference; that they were no more than playthings, the stars' tennis balls, knocked hither and thither. And from this it followed that the gods themselves lost at Ping-Pong, choked on the big points, and suffered from back trouble and the thousands of other aches and pains – pulled muscles, sprained ankles, colds – that the flesh is heir to.

It worked the other way too, this waterfall-induced idea of the chain of being. Nietzsche said that there could not possibly be a god; if there were, then how could he bear not to be one? On the infinite edge, it seemed to me, you could be a god and it would not actually make any difference; you might not even know you *were* one.

By the time we got to Sayan Terrace, months later, my back was in perfect shape again. I had regained my virility and I no longer felt like an infirm old man or an old god with a bad back. Gregor and I designed a game. We stood at the edge of the pool and threw a tennis ball back and forth, taking it in turns to stand on the overflow edge. It was a new kind of game, one that made competition a form of cooperation. The most important thing was not to lose the ball, not to drop it, not to cast it into the void. If you made a throw that the other person failed to catch, then you both lost. Either you both won or you both lost. This meant that the thrower had to throw accurately. At the same time, it was boring for the catcher if the thrower presented him with catches that were too easy. The catcher wanted to make spectacular catches. So we threw the ball back and forth, harder and harder, sometimes straight at the other person's face or at the limit of his reach. When you were catching you had to make sure that, as well as catching the ball, you didn't topple backwards, especially if you were on the infinite edge. We did all this in absolute silence so that the other loungers and bathers would have no cause for complaint. In fact, I think they enjoyed watching us. Their heads swivelled left and right like spectators at Wimbledon. We had become part of the view. Circle was watching us, of course. Her man was not an old man with a bad back, he was a virile man showing off, unperturbed by the ominous tweak of a muscle in his lower back.

Whenever possible I caught the ball one-handed and threw it back hard. The idea was to make the other person almost drop the ball, to make him almost topple over the infinite edge. Gregor had his back to the gorge and sent the ball screaming back to me. It smacked into my right hand. There was something profoundly satisfying about feeling the ball smack safely into the palm like this. I threw it back as hard as I could with my left hand. Gregor caught it an inch from his face. He threw it back and I had to strain upwards to catch it – just – in my left hand. Gregor, who must have known I was partial to people quoting Rilke, said: '*Ach der geworfene, ach der gewagte Ball, füllt er die Hände nicht anders mit Wiederkehr: rein um sein Heimgewicht ist er mehr.*'

Behind him was the gorge, the infinite edge. The ball was a yellow planet spinning back and forth through the blue sky. We were in a trance of throwing and catching. It could not go on for ever but we never knew when the game was going to end, and so, at any one moment, it lasted for ever.

SKUNK

In April 1999 I spent several days in Paris researching a 'walk' for the *Time Out Book of Paris Walks*. My walk was in the eleventh arrondissement, where I had lived, off and on, for much of the early nineties, but I was actually staying with my friends Hervé and Mimi in the eighth, on rue de l'Elysée, opposite the presidential palace. For dinner on the evening of my arrival, Hervé said, he had invited a new friend of theirs, a beautiful young woman called Marie Roget.

When Marie arrived she was, if not beautiful in the way Mimi is, extremely attractive. She was tall (almost six foot) with calm green eyes and what, from my cheaply barbered point of view (fifty rupees, in Goa), seemed expensively styled black hair. Although dressed like a gas pump attendant on a space station – her trousers, manufactured from some ultra-synthetic heat- and cold-resistant fabric, consisted entirely of pockets – she had a Parisian fondness for debate and strident argument. When, during the course of dinner, I declared myself 'totally pro-NATO, a hundred per cent in favour of bombing Serbia', she found it incredible that 'a so-called intellectual could say – let alone think – something so stupid'.

'Who said I was an intellectual?' I said.

'Hervé,' she said.

'Ah, he must have been teasing,' I said.

I liked her even though she smoked a great deal, more than Hervé and Mimi, who are fairly heavy smokers. After dinner, drunk, I dropped a wine glass. As we cleared up the curves and splinters of glass, Marie cut her finger and a few drops of blood landed on my battered trainers. She ran her hand under the cold tap in the bathroom and I wrapped a Band-Aid around her long slim finger – an action which alluded, however medically, to the possibility of marriage. The atmosphere between us changed, softened, and we arranged to meet the following day so that we could research my walk together. She wrote her number on the last page of my notebook, leaving a faint smear of blood as she did so. Her handwriting was bold, unambiguous.

'Call me after lunch,' she said as we kissed goodbye.

Hervé was leaving Paris the following afternoon to visit a friend in Marseille. We met for lunch on his way to the Gare de Lyon, in a restaurant in the eleventh, where I had spent the morning researching my walk. Hervé insisted – as he did about all the women he introduced me to – that Marie was dying to go to bed with me. I insisted – as I always do – that he was wrong, that in any case, of all the women he had introduced me to, there was only one I wanted to go to bed with, and that was Mimi. After we had said goodbye I called Marie and we arranged to meet at the Café Charbon on Oberkampf.

She turned up exactly on time, wearing black combat trousers and a pale T-shirt with something Japanese written on the front. So, she said after we had taken a coffee (my fourth of the day), what did I want to do? I said that it would be very useful for my walk if we could get stoned. Marie was happy to try, even though grass never had any effect on her.

We spent a long time trying to find a place where we could discreetly get high. In one little park there were too many mothers and young children who might have thought we were junkies; in another, too many young kids who we thought were junkies. There were windows, eyes, everywhere. Eventually we found a bench by the Canal Saint Martin. Evidently this was quite a spot for stoners; on the next bench along, a couple were already smoking a joint. As I filled a pipe Marie said again that she had tried several times to smoke grass but it never had any effect on her.

'Oh well, let's hope this does,' I said. Although we had only met the night before, I felt perfectly relaxed with her, possibly because I had no sexual feelings towards her. This was partly because she smoked cigarettes, partly because I had a girlfriend in England (though I did not mention this, of course). I don't know if she had any kind of sexual feelings for me. Probably not – I had learned long ago to set no store by anything Hervé said in this regard – but I think she was curious because I did not fit any of the moulds from which Parisian men were cast. This was the first afternoon she had spent with a forty-year-old intellectual who had nothing intelligent to say about – and little interest in – anything except nightclubs and smoking dope. I lit the pipe, took a couple of hits, and passed it to her. It was obvious that although she smoked cigarettes continually, she had no idea how to do this.

'Hold it in,' I said, coughing, 'for as long as you can.' She tried again, passed the pipe back to me, and breathed out. I took another big hit and passed the pipe to her again. A barge was going through a lock on the canal. The effort of negotiating these locks seemed so enormous as to take all the fun out of travelling by canal. I was glad that I was sitting here watching, getting stoned, rather than becoming actively involved in the interminable chore of lock negotiation, but I would have preferred not even to have seen it. I was surprised how quickly I was high.

'Are you feeling anything yet?' I said.

'No. Are you?'

'I'm completely blasted,' I said.

'What is it like?'

'It's difficult to say. Like being stoned. It's not like anything else.'

We walked a little further, unsure of where we were going because of the profound – some would say disturbing – spatial disorientation that is a characteristic of skunk. I was noticing everything, but as soon as I noticed one thing, I noticed something else, and so, in a way, I was oblivious to everything. We were no longer by the canal, we were walking along a street jammed with cars, parked and moving, though even the moving cars were stationary. The dull sky had brightened slightly. Marie waited outside while I went into a shop – our mouths were terribly dry – and bought a couple of bottles of Evian.

'Feeling anything?' I asked. The water was so cold it made my teeth hurt.

'I feel funny.'

'How?'

'I don't think I like it.'

'D'you feel ill?'

'No, but I—'

'Don't worry about it. Just enjoy it.'

'What was that stuff you gave me?'

'Grass.'

'No. It can't have been.'

'It was. Skunk. Very strong grass. But you only had a little, so don't worry.' I took her by the arm, smiled, and we walked along like a nice Parisian couple out for a stroll. If we could get through the next few minutes I was confident we would have a good time. We had not been strolling for long, though, when Marie said she wanted to sit down. There was a café over the road so we crossed, carefully, and sat down at an outside table.

'Where are we?' she said.

'I don't know. Rue something . . .' I looked around but could not see a sign.

'Where are we?' she said again.

'Paris. In a café. Quite a nice café,' I said. 'A Parisian café, if you will.' Walking had meant that Marie was not able to focus entirely on how weird she was feeling. Now that we were seated, however, there was nothing to distract her.

'Would you like something to drink?' I said.

'What was that stuff you gave me?'

'Grass. Just grass,' I said, though whether this was strictly true is a moot point. Many people regard skunk as a genetically modified product and boycott it accordingly.

Marie shook her head. 'Why did you do this?'

'Do what?'

'Give me that stuff.'

'I thought it would be fun. And useful for my work.'

'Why?'

'It enables one to enter the Zone,' I said. 'You know, the dream space of the city.'

'Why do you want to do that?'

'It's a version of the city I like.'

'I don't want to be in your city. I want to be in my city. Where is my city? Why can't we be in my city?'

The waiter came over. I ordered two coffees even though, as well as being bombed on skunk, I was already feeling wired from too much coffee. When the waiter had gone, Marie, looking pale, asked, 'Why me?'

'What do you mean?'

'Of all the people in Paris, why me? Why me?'

'Because I met you yesterday and I thought you were cool. I thought we could hang out, research my walk. I thought it would be fun.' She shook her head, which was, in a way, fair comment. It was obvious that she was not having fun. Far from it. She did not know where she was. Who she was. Even *if* she was. Skunk is like that, especially for the first twenty minutes or so, which can be like pandemonium. That's why people who like it – people like me – like it.

'What have you done to me?'

'Listen, it's only grass. However strange you're feeling, it can't have any bad effect on you physically. If I had given you a pill, let's say, and you began feeling funny, then I would be worried because maybe it could have some physical consequences. But this is only grass. It's physically harmless. It's just in your head. If you relax and go with it, it will be fine. It will be nice.'

She shook her head. The waiter came back with the coffees neither of us wanted. He glanced at Marie and saw, I think, that all was not quite well. I was totally out of it too but intent on behaving properly, on saying and doing all the right things, on trying to reassure her.

After a while she said, 'You're not really with *Time Out*, are you?'

'Of course I am.'

'Who sent you?' she said abruptly, and with such vehemence that it sounded like a line from a thriller.

'That is a line you utter,' I said, 'while grabbing someone by the lapels and shoving them up against the wall of a garbage-strewn alley. It's a line to be hissed, your face inches from the person you're hissing at. "Who sent you? Who sent you?"' This little speech made no impression on her and so, smirking slightly, I added, '*Time Out* sent me.'

My notebook was on the table. She picked it up and began looking through the scrawled notes I had made for my contribution to the *Time Out Book of Paris Walks*. My handwriting is impossible for anyone else to read – I have trouble reading it myself sometimes – but she was staring intently at every page.

'You're not writing a guide at all,' she said, a look of vacant realization in her green eyes.

'Of course I am.'

'You're putting me in a novel, aren't you?' she said, each new page confirming her suspicions. Still inwardly smirking, I shook my head. She shook hers too and turned to the last page of the book, the page with people's phone numbers.

'Why do you have all these numbers?'

'They're people I know in Paris, people I hoped to have time to see.'

'Why is my number here?'

'You wrote it in there yesterday,' I said, relieved that she appeared not to have noticed the dried smudge of blood. She took a Biro from her bag – the same Biro she had used the day before – and began trying to cross out her name and number. Unfortunately the pen had run out of ink since then, and so she began using it as a chisel, gashing out parts of that page and the three or four underneath. It was a gesture of self-obliteration, almost of suicide. The sight of all those telephone numbers had put another idea in her head as well.

'I need to make a call,' she said. For some time now I had realized that she was not the adventurous free spirit she had seemed the day before. But when she said this, when she said she wanted to make a call, I saw that she was someone who often spent evenings hanging out on the phone, chatting to friends, many of whom had boyfriends and did not live near by. I could feel the loneliness, the skunk loneliness that was now overwhelming her. At the same time, she had seen something in me.

'You are evil,' she said. Skunk is like that: it takes the normal dope smoker's paranoia and raises it to a level of reeling expressionist insight. This is not without its plus points. You feel the paranoia so palpably, even in situations in which there is no threat or danger, that skunk offers a chance to experience it in uniquely pure, uncut form – as dread, almost – with no anchoring in external events. Or at least that is what I used to think. I have since stopped smoking skunk because it made me too paranoid.

'Please listen,' I said. 'Trust me. I know that's what you feel you can't do, but you must trust me. I promise that nothing bad will happen to you.' I reached for her hand and she did not snatch it away. I held it the way you hold the hand of an injured or dying person, not as you take the hand of a young woman in a Paris café you are on the brink of making a pass at. While I was speaking she seemed to be listening, but as soon as I stopped she was off again.

'I have to make a call,' she said. This was not a good idea for several reasons. To get to the phone she would have to walk into the bar, possibly ask the barman where the phone was. Any friend she called would be alarmed at the way she sounded, the way she didn't know where she was, the way she was with this sinister English intellectual she barely knew. The friend would ask to speak to the barman, and before we knew it we would be in trouble – and keeping us both out of trouble was my main concern.

'How about this?' I said. 'You sit here and I'll phone Mimi. She knows us both. She will reassure you.' Marie shook her head. Determined to have her way and make a call, she stood up. I was torn between physically restraining her – thereby making her more frightened, possibly creating a commotion – and . . .

It was too late anyway. She was walking into the bar. I watched her disappear into the back of the café, relieved that she did not have any communication with the barman. Now that she was gone I was aware of how hard I had been concentrating on acting normally, reasonably. I was feeling the effort of trying to remain calm as a physical sensation, of extreme tension, in my head. I wanted to behave correctly – to do the

73

right thing, as they say – but another part of me was becoming a little irritated that my afternoon's research was being so thoroughly fucked up.

After a few minutes Marie came back. As she did, for the first time that day the sun came out. She had not made a call because she could not remember anyone's number. Good, I thought. Thank heavens for small blessings. And since sitting down had not made her feel any better, it seemed a good idea to resume our abortive stroll. I left forty francs on the table for our untouched coffees and we got up. Unfortunately, walking presented her with new problems. Out of the corner of her eye she kept seeing things – a black dog whose tail had been chopped off, a butcher's shop full of pink meat, a torso of kebab in a Greek restaurant – things she didn't like, things that made her frightened. One of these things was me. Which is why, presumably, she announced that she wanted to take a taxi. This threw into even sharper relief the same dilemma that had confronted me when she had wanted to make a phone call. She may have been freaking out, but while she was under my custodianship, even though she was having a terrible time, nothing could happen to her. However bad she was feeling, she was better off under my protection. While I was thinking this she hailed a taxi. The taxi pulled over. She opened the door and began getting in. I could have pulled her out of the taxi, I could have got in the taxi myself, but she was in the taxi and I was standing on the pavement and I had done neither. I bent down and glanced at the driver. She pulled the door to and they drove off. One moment the taxi was there, at the kerb, and the next moment there was just the kerb and the oil-stained road and the shops opposite.

For a few moments I was relieved that she was gone. Then I became worried that she would not remember where she lived. No sooner had I thought this than I became convinced that the driver was going to abduct, rape or kill her. I could imagine the scene in the car as vividly as if I were there, as if mine were the eyes she saw in the driver's mirror, glancing at her as she sat rigid, white, clutching her bag, heading through the city which no longer had any direction or familiarity. It seemed certain that in the course of the next couple of days her body – her partly clothed body, as they say – would be discovered in the Bois de Boulogne. Stupidly, I had neglected to check the licence plate.

I walked for a few minutes and then stopped at a café where the floor had just been cleaned. A smell of ammonia filled the place. I ordered my sixth coffee of the day and went to the toilet where I avoided making eye contact with the mirror. My penis, as happens when I am nervous or stoned or have drunk too much coffee (all three on this occasion), had shrunk dramatically: it was nothing but wrinkled foreskin, and I found it difficult to piss. Then, when I had finished pissing, I found it difficult to stop completely. I should have got in the taxi with her. I kept replaying that moment, the moment when it was possible to have acted differently, but the outcome was always the same.

When I returned to my table I made a few notes of things she had said, in case one day I wanted to use what had happened in a book. I had a sharp sense of her in the taxi, of the driver's eyes and the neon dread of the city as it sped past. By now they had been driving for quite a time, but her apartment was not getting any nearer. She couldn't tell which *quartier* she was in. Everywhere looked like everywhere else, and nowhere looked like anywhere. I turned to the back of the notebook where she had erased her name and number. Seeing the brown smear of blood, I remembered the drops that had fallen on to my trainers. I looked down at them but they were so grubby that the incriminating blood would only be forensically apparent. I deliberately asked the waiter, in English, where we were, what time it was. I got him to point out where we were in my *Plan de Paris*. I made sure that he would remember me. My mouth was drier than ever.

Before leaving, I called Mimi and explained what had happened. She said she would phone Marie at her apartment. Unsure what else to do, I continued researching my walk. I walked down Popincourt (the street where I used to live) and Basfroi to rue de Charonne, which, oddly, was quite deserted. The building on the corner had not been renovated since the time of Atget and looked, consequently, as if it had been squatted by ghosts. Remembering what Walter Benjamin had said of Atget – that he photographed Paris as if it were the scene of a crime – I walked down Keller back to rue de la Roquette. Twilight was falling. People were hurrying and strolling, heading home or going out or just lingering. All the bars and café terraces were full of Parisians smoking and drinking, and the street was crowded too. Glad to be among people again, I mingled with the crowd, looking in shop windows, heading in the direction of the Bastille.

At nine o'clock I met a friend for dinner at Chez Paul

and then took the Métro back to the eighth. As I entered rue de l'Elysée, a gendarme asked where I was going. This always happens, because of the proximity of the presidential palace. Remaining calm, I explained that I was staying with friends who lived at number 20, and he waved me on.

Mimi answered the door wearing a white bathrobe. She had just washed her hair and wrapped it in a thick turban of towel. I had hoped that by now Marie would have called, saying that she was at home and feeling better, but there had been no response to the message left by Mimi. I suggested calling again but Mimi said not to worry, Marie would probably call in the morning, a little embarrassed, but perfectly OK.

'Yes,' I said, but it seemed equally likely that if we did get a call, it would be the police saying everything was far from OK.

Mimi had just opened a bottle of red wine. I filled a glass for myself and told her in more detail about what had happened. I emphasized the funny side and drew attention to how correctly I had behaved. Basically, I made light of the whole episode. Mimi sat on the sofa. Her toenails were painted a lovely pale green. I took my shoes off – what with one thing and another I had been on the trudge practically all day – and stretched out on the seat opposite with my feet on the coffee table. From this low angle I could see a crescent moon, hanging above the presidential palace as though an Islamic republic had been proclaimed. This impression was enhanced when Mimi got up and played a record of an old man singing in Arabic – it was a goatherd's lament, I think. She dried her hair vigorously and then hung the towel in the bathroom and sat on the sofa again, her legs curled under her. Her hair was still damp. I poured more wine. I had just glanced at the clock – it was almost twelve-thirty – when the phone rang.

YOGA FOR PEOPLE
WHO CAN'T BE BOTHERED
TO DO IT

Kate's grandfather died in the fighting – the savage fighting – on Saipan (at least I *think* it was Saipan) in July 1943. He was in the first wave of landing craft to hit the beach. He survived the landing and the subsequent battle only to be killed later by a booby trap when the island had been secured. The invasion took place the morning after the night of the full moon. In a letter written sometime after the landing, he told Kate's grandmother how he had spent part of that night on the deck of the troopship. It was nice, he said, knowing that the moon shining on him was shining on her too, back in Philadelphia. I don't know if this is true. I mean, does the fact that the moon is full in one part of the world mean that it's full elsewhere, or is there some kind of cosmic lag? Irrespective of the astronomy, I liked the way that – like many before and since – he had found solace in the idea of the universal moon. You might say it is a cliché but, as Borges pointed out, there are only half a dozen big metaphors, so it's not surprising that we keep coming back to them. In Kate's grandfather's last letter he said that he had never felt 'so intensely alive' as he had during the invasion and its aftermath.

As well as these sea-smudged letters there is also footage of the landing, some of the first shot in colour, drenched in Iwo Jima blue. Kate's grandfather is not featured in the footage but his buddies are. You can see the white wake spreading out victoriously behind the landing craft, the palm-fringed beach, the marine – as in USMC – blue of the sea. It's silent, but the flick-a-flick of the film moving through the projector is like the memory of the drone of the motors, the smack of waves. If you see it on TV that same flick-a-flick is latent in the intense saturation of colour. You can see the waves breaking on the beach and the men looking forward, dry-mouthed, to the moment when they hit the beach and it is just a roll of the dice whether they will live or die or end up maimed between the two for the rest of their days. Kate's father was five at the time and it is surprising to me that he did not grow up to be a crew-cut obsessive devoting all his energy to learning everything he could about the war in the Pacific and the exact gory circumstances of his father's death. But he didn't turn out like that, he turned out normal and kind, and Kate was his daughter.

I had been travelling in Southeast Asia for a month when I met her, at the Sanctuary on Ko Pha-Ngan. The Sanctuary was a resort of sorts, two beaches around from Haad Rin, accessible either by an exhausting two-hour yomp over mountainous, snake-infested jungle or by a pleasant, twenty-minute boat ride. You could learn poi at the Sanctuary or Thai massage or do yoga or just swim in the sea or laze around and look forward to the big full-moon parties in Haad Rin. The bungalows – huts really – were very simple, tucked into the edge of the frightening jungle, but the bar and restaurant area, overlooking the beach, strewn with hammocks and Thai cushions, was idyllic. During the day it was breezy and cool; in the evenings it was lit by soft amber lanterns. There was also an excellent library with editions of Auden and Blake as well as the expected volumes of Castaneda and Tao-of-crystal-healing stuff.

I had arrived at the Sanctuary a week before the monthly full-moon party at Haad Rin. Haad Rin may have been nice once, not long ago, but now it was choked by its own popularity, full of beautiful ravers who watched loud movies on TV during the day and waited for the fluoro night. I went over there every couple of days to check my e-mail; other than that I didn't stray far from the Sanctuary. After weeks of hectic travel, hauling my rucksack on and off trains, visiting temples – ruined and still intact – and checking in and out of guesthouses every other day, I was happy lying in a hammock or propped on one of those triangular Thai cushions that I have never found comfortable (even the serenely reclining Buddha looks like his neck could do with more support).

On my first afternoon I met Jake from Austin, Texas. Feeling very much like a self-conscious new arrival, I was relieved when he introduced himself and sat down next to me on the beach. He had rock-star hair and biker tattoos – women, a dagger, serpents – down his back and arms. Actually, pretty much everyone on Ko Pha-Ngan had some kind of tattoo; you tended to notice people who *didn't* have one, but Jake's were not easily overlooked. I asked him about them and he told me what they signified, but as far as I could see most of them signified nothing but their own ugliness. The last one he'd had done – a rose bursting into flame – was slightly nicer and symbolised redemption from the bad things he'd done in his past (like getting himself covered in repulsive tattoos). He had changed his entire belief system since then, he said as we sat on the beach, pouring coarse sand through our fingers. Now he was 'into the whole self-journey thing'.

In this respect Jake lagged somewhat behind Troy (a single tattoo of a small bird on his left shoulder blade), a very handsome and fit-looking guy who walked around the whole time. I have, at various times, gone through some fairly distracted phases myself, but even at my worst I never fidgeted the way Troy did. He never sat down for more than a few seconds – which was strange since both feet were wrapped in bandages and walking evidently caused him considerable discomfort. His left hand was also bandaged, and were it not for the absence of bandages on his right hand you could have been forgiven for thinking that he had been crucified. I am always curious about people's injuries – every scar is a story – and asked him what had happened to his feet.

'Bad karma,' he said.

'How do you mean?'

'I got these blisters on my feet.'

'So why is that bad karma?'

'Memories. A lot of memories came out.'

'Out of your *feet*?'

'A lot of bad memories.' With that he was up and off, in the sense that he left me, sat down somewhere else for a few minutes, and then was up and off again. When we spoke the next day he mentioned his time 'in the hospital'. My ears pricked up.

'For your feet?' I asked innocently.

'No, for this,' he said, knocking his head.

'Something you'd taken?' (On the night of the full-moon parties, I had heard, extra psychiatric staff were taken on at the nearby hospital for people who went bananas on mushrooms, acid, E, or a combination plate of all three.)

'Yes.'

'What did you take?' (I like hearing stories about people getting messed up on drugs.)

'Oh, scorpion venom. All sorts of other things.' He'd been into a form of meditation that requires you to concentrate on your dead body decomposing in the earth; from there he moved on to kamikaze tai chi and God knows what else: the extreme wing of all the self-journeying stuff that people try out when they're in this part of the world. His teacher, a French-Canadian, had taken him down this route, feeding him all sorts of shamanic eye-of-newt, tongue-of-frog stuff. At one point, said Troy, he even drank a bottle of poison. I imagined a bottle with a skull and cross-bones on it and POISON in stencilled letters.

'Why d'you do that?' I asked.

'I wanted to experience mortality. Death. What would happen if I died? Nothing. I'd just come back in some other form. I have vivid memories of being a tree. A stone. A river. Water. We are water.'

'Sure,' I said, taking a gulp of mineral water, a gulp, that is to say, of myself. After a certain point in his self-journeying Troy couldn't remember anything. Next thing he knew he was in the psychiatric ward.

'How was that?'

'Oh it was . . . It was . . .' He stood up and walked

85

around, sat down, stood up and came back. Since he was reluctant or unable to continue his narrative beyond this point, I asked him about the studies he had alluded to in a previous conversation. What had he studied, back in America, before getting into all this wild stuff?

'First, business. My father was a businessman.' I was surprised how often I heard this from Americans. They did this or that because their father had done it. I had met people in England who went to the same Oxford college as their father, but there did not seem to be this same compulsion to do what your father had done simply because it was what your father had done.

'I didn't like business,' Troy continued. 'It wasn't really me. So then I did literature. I studied that.' I loved that 'that': it made literature sound like something you did in the same way that you did a scuba-diving course, after which you would be given a PADI certificate that meant you were qualified to swim in the open waters of Melville or Conrad.

'But it's here that I've really learned a lot,' Troy continued. 'I've learned about pain. That's why we're all here, to confront pain. To heal ourselves.'

I had some problems with this. Although I liked the atmosphere of the Sanctuary – and of almost any alternative, New Age-inflected place – the emphasis on healing was implicitly predicated on the idea of sickness and injury. It ended up replicating the fall. Actually, as I looked around, I saw that several people here *were* ill. Maybe they'd become ill as a precondition of being healed. Whichever way you looked at it, quite a few people had gone down with some kind of stomach upset. Marian, a gaunt-looking Dutch woman, said it was a means of 'purification'. I thought it sounded like dysentery. On the beach one day I looked across and saw a woman vomiting into the sand. In addition to the inevitable stomach upsets, everyone had cut their toes on coral or sharp bits of stone. I kept my Tevas on whenever possible, was even a little reluctant to take them off to paddle through the footbath that was used to wash sand off your feet before you entered the Sanctuary. I worried about catching a verruca or picking up some of the bad memories that had come out of Troy's feet. (For a while I contemplated writing a story about someone who absorbs other people's memories, memories of their friends and the things that have happened to them, memories that become intermingled with his own; then I realized that the person was me and I had already written several stories like that.) I also took great pains not to get ill, to avoid an accident such as that suffered by poor Gareth, who had been stung by jellyfish.

He was an intense, shy, lumbering English fellow and he had swum into a little school of jellyfish. Even though he was a strong swimmer – he told me later that it was his ambition to swim the Channel – the shock had nearly made him drown, he said. He still looked stunned by it, but he was the kind of guy who probably looked stunned anyway. As part of his convalescence he lay in a hammock for large parts of the day, reading Blake, the prophetic books. He also played a lot of chess with Jake, who, Gareth reckoned, was one of the best chess players he had ever met. Jake was a jailhouse chess master, lacking sophistication but confounding more techni- cally accomplished players with his devil-may-care aggression, resorting, on occasion, to moves that were on the edge of legality. Gareth, by contrast, was a sullen plodder, contemplating his options with a concentration full of heavy foreboding.

There were quite a few people who liked to play chess and several more who liked to play backgammon, which Jake was also good at. One time he asked me if I wanted to play and I explained that I didn't like to do anything that involved concentrating. I didn't even do yoga. I was practically the only person who didn't. A lot of people did yoga even when they weren't actually doing it. They were always stretching or bending or just sitting in quite demanding positions. Everyone had perfect posture and walked as though gravity were an option rather than a law. I wished I'd been doing yoga for years – in fact I'd been wishing I'd been doing yoga for years for years – but I was incapable of starting. I ended up not even reading, just hanging out, smoking grass, or chatting to people like Wayne, a Robert Stone character who was writing a memoir of his life in America back in the sixties and seventies. Since the bungalows at the Sanctuary had electricity only between six and eleven in the evening, Wayne spent most of the day waiting for his laptop to charge up.

'You know how I got round the draft?' he asked me during one of these long, powerless interludes.

When I shook my head he saluted me. Along the base of his right hand, in faded black ink, was tattooed FUCK YOU.

'That's insubordination,' I said.

'You got it, bro,' he said.

I had settled in nicely at the Sanctuary, felt quite at home and in great shape, mentally and physically. So much so that I resolved to walk through the jungle, over the mountain to Haad Rin. The jungle rustled and scurried with ominousness. Every branch and rock exuded snake. It was hilly, bouldery, wobbly with rocks, crawling with serpentine vegetation. After a quarter of an hour I was relieved to see a slender French guy walking the other way – towards the Sanctuary – who said that from here on the path got worse. The jungle closed in, you walked through low corridors of spooky vegetation. I hesitated for a few moments, told myself that I was being feeble – and followed him back to the aptly named Sanctuary.

Even there, though, I did not feel a hundred per cent safe. One night a wild animal jumped through the glassless window of my hut while I was asleep. It was only a cat but I lay awake for hours afterwards, hearing creatures prowl and scurry through their encroached-upon wilderness. Troy had seen a snake. So had Wayne. I hoped I wouldn't. I was also worried about jellyfish, obviously, and went swimming only with other people, people like Heidi, a Canadian living in Singapore, and Rob from San Francisco, both of whom were strong swimmers. Heidi demonstrated her ability to float on her back, effortlessly, legs and arms outstretched. Like this, she said, you could stay afloat for hours, possibly days, awaiting rescue. The key – as in all such matters – is to relax totally, but it is very difficult to will yourself into a state of absolute relaxation. Rob couldn't manage it for long and I couldn't manage it at all.

A long way out, we could see someone swimming. They were so far out all we could see was a rock of hair surrounded by the flatness of the sea. It wouldn't have looked so bad if there had been two people, but the fact that it was just someone on their own – prone to sudden cramp, weird currents, and shark attacks – made them seem even further out than they really were. The three of us had a brief debate about swimming so far from the shore. Heidi thought it extremely stupid and Rob agreed. Although I am a very timid swimmer I took a more indulgent view.

'If they're that far out,' I said, 'they must feel confident about being able to get back, so in terms of what they're capable of, maybe they're not far out at all. There is not an absolute standard for these things. Take me, for instance. I'm already feeling out of my depth even though I could stand on the bottom if I wanted to – which I won't do, of course, in case I cut my feet on something.'

'If anything happened they'd be in trouble,' said Rob, and as we looked at that small head it seemed already, inherently, at risk. Whoever it was out there was way out of shouting range, so far out I was not sure we would even notice if anything happened. You could look away for a few minutes and when you looked back the head would no longer be there and the change in what you saw would be almost insignificant.

We hung around in the water, chatting. The sea was flat and warm, room temperature, really. A long-tail boat pulled into the bay, churning up the water and the silence, bouncing noise off the bay and the mountain, leaving a clanging emptiness in its wake. A law of acoustics, something pertaining to sound and water and echoes – the scientific principle behind sonar, say – had been made briefly audible. It seemed a good moment to head back to the beach, where Jake was practising fire-free poi. A woman in a red bikini, gorgeous, had also got out of the sea, fractionally ahead of us.

'I've been *stung*,' she was saying, to Jake specifically, but she was also just saying it – 'I've been *stung*' – to anyone, saying it because of the shock and pain, which were indistinguishable from each other and making each other worse. Her arms and stomach were blotched as red as her bikini.

Without stopping his spinning Jake said, 'Vinegar.'

'What?' she said.

'Use vinegar.' She was standing there, arms held out as if they were sticky, in terrible shock, but once she understood what Jake meant she hurried into the Sanctuary.

'That's who was swimming so far out,' said Rob.

'No!'

'Definitely.'

'A parable has been enacted before our eyes,' I said. 'But the question still remains – was she swimming too far out? Yes, in the sense that perhaps she would not have got stung if she'd been closer to the shore. No, in the sense that in spite of getting stung, she still made it back to shore.' Rob was very easy to be with but there were times when I did not quite have the patience to enter into a dialogue with him. I preferred to assume the roles of both parties in a conversation of which he was a mute witness.

At dinner I made sure I was well placed to get all the gory details about the incident from the woman who had been stung. The jellyfish were translucent, brownish red, the same ones that had afflicted poor Gareth. They – dozens of them, an armada, a fleet – had stung her arms and stomach. She had swum back in a dreadful state, afraid that she would have to make her way through more of them, swimming in such a way as to protect her face. She had felt the venom, or whatever it was, spreading through her arms, which were terribly blotchy still. Over some of the worst stings she had stuck little pieces of paper. She was eating a huge barracuda steak that looked even bigger because she was so slim. On another plate she had a mound of mashed potatoes. She was in shock but she was already recovering. I watched her eat and talk. She went from looking plain to beautiful three or four times a minute. I couldn't stop looking at her as she flickered back and forth, but beneath all of this was the steady, unambiguous beauty of her freedom, of the reserves of strength and independence that were so much greater than anything she had needed that afternoon, greater than anything that had yet happened to her. As I looked at her I realized that, for me, the sensation of falling for a woman is often touched with this conviction that she will never need me. I wasn't sure what I was feeling, and then the familiarity of this particular aspect of the process – a side-effect almost – made me recognize it, made me realize that, yes, I was falling for her. Appropriately enough, I experienced this as a kind of vertigo – a species of Victorian swoon – induced by the discrepancy between the yearning I felt for her and the hunch that she was not feeling anything of the kind for me. As soon as she had finished her steak-sized chunk of barracuda she said goodnight to everyone and went to bed.

'To lick my wounds,' she said.

That, I hardly need explain, was how I met Kate.

When I saw her again, the following morning, she looked much better. There were still some welts on her arms but the shock had worked its way through her system. We talked again about the incident and its aftermath.

'The worst thing was in the shower,' she said. 'I was

shampooing my hair. I had this absolute need to shampoo my hair thoroughly. I was covered in lather and the water ran out. So I was covered in jellyfish stings and covered in shampoo lather and I was suddenly freezing and I cried my eyes out. It was the shampoo that made me cry.'

'Did the water come on again?' I said.

'Eventually. After about half an hour.'

'Did that half an hour seem like an eternity?' I said.

'I just sat on my bed, sobbing.'

'Then you came down and ate that barracuda steak, right? I loved that. It was like you were taking a kind of ravenous revenge on the ocean and all who dwelt in it.'

'I was hungry. I really needed to eat.'

'The venom was coursing through you,' I said. 'Triggering all sorts of strange reactions. The body was struggling to cope. It needed fuel.'

'I had strange dreams in the night.'

'Sea dreams?'

'Yes. Drowning dreams.'

'We saw you swimming. Rob and Heidi thought you were too far out.'

'What about you?'

'I felt ambiguous about it. You *were* a long way out. But it was up to you. And then, when you got out of the water . . .'

'Yes?'

'I had two really powerful reactions when I saw you standing there.'

'What were they?'

'I'll tell you what they were, but if it's OK, I won't tell you the order in which they occurred.'

'OK.'

'One was overwhelming relief that it was you that got stung and not me.'

'And the other?'

'That you looked absolutely gorgeous in your red bikini.'

'Bubble-gum pink.'

'In your bubble-gum pink bikini.'

At breakfast the next day, the day of the full-moon party in Haad Rin, Kate suggested to Gareth that they swim around the bay to the beach at Haad Yuan.

'You know,' she said, 'a kind of get-back-on-that-horse kind of thing.' Gareth agreed, naturally. He was so cumbersome, socially and physically, and she moved through the world with such ease and confidence, that I guessed he was probably utterly in love with her. He must have been accustomed to people taking little interest in him, their attention always drifting towards other, more attractive individuals, and here was this beautiful woman in her red – her bubble-gum pink – bikini, proposing that they swim to Haad Yuan together. She asked me if I wanted to come but I am a very weak swimmer and, though tempted, I was frightened of jellyfish and worried that I might get stung or drown or both. There are many ways I don't want to die, and drowning is one of them.

Before they set off Kate tucked forty baht into her bikini bottom. 'For refreshments,' she said.

I watched them walk down the beach. She was thin and lovely and he was heavy and cumbersome, but in the water this would turn to buoyancy and confidence. They waded into the glinting sea and then they began swimming and disappeared around the headland.

What did I do while they were gone? Nothing probably. I had got into a state of some kind of bliss at the Sanctuary. Normally I am shifting from one moment to another, fidgeting like Troy, never quite being still, always aware of something that I would rather be doing, but at the Sanctuary I sat happily in my skin whatever I was doing. I drifted in and out of conversations with people who came and went on boats or who walked into the sea. Tammy and John – a Canadian couple who, several years later, I would camp with at Black Rock City – stopped by while I ate a mung bean curry for lunch. Like me, John was wearing one of those DIESEL: ULTRA-VIOLENT SKINBLOCK T-shirts which were on sale everywhere in Thailand at that time. Wayne and I saluted each other (it had become something of a routine by now) and Troy gave me a progress report on the state of his feet, which were getting better even though they still looked a right old mess. That was another nice thing about the Sanctuary: hanging out at certain spots indicated that you were available for conversation, but there were other, more secluded places where you were always left to your own devices. Personally, I had no need of solitude; I'd had enough of it for one lifetime and always sat where there was a chance of some passing conversational trade. After Troy had gone a dog came and did some yoga. I looked at the sea, dozed, and glanced at whatever book I was not reading. All I was really doing, though, was waiting for Kate to get back, hoping she would not be long.

She came back soon after lunch. So did Gareth. Kate pulled up a chair next to me, and Gareth sat down too. It had been a perfect swim. There had been no current, and although they had kept an eye out for jellyfish, the thought of them had not diminished the pleasure of swimming. They were both gleaming with water. I noticed, for the first time, that Kate had a white ink tattoo of the Om symbol on her shoulder. She ordered lunch – a huge portion of pad thai. Jake came and sat with us too.

When I was younger I had a predatory attitude to women, but these days I could no longer bear the exertion, the stress, the single-mindedness it required. I was trying to be passive, to put myself at the mercy of events rather than willing them to happen. I tried, as the four of us sat there, not to do any of the things that I dislike men doing when they are obviously interested in a woman. I tried not to talk too much, tried not to try to impress, tried to talk to Gareth and Jake rather than directing all my attention at Kate. I listened but tried not to listen with that 'Look how hard I'm listening' look on my face to which I am sometimes prone (especially if I'm not listening). And yet, however hard I tried to take a disinterested, even sceptical view of things, it *did* seem that Kate was leaning towards me, that I was getting slightly more than my fair share of her attention, that her eyes, whenever I looked her way, were always there, waiting to meet mine. It was like those odd occasions when you are playing cards and are dealt one good hand after another. It may be luck but it feels like the opposite, it feels like destiny. Everything falls into place and nothing requires any effort. We both loved *Voyager* with Sam Shepard and Julie Delpy, a film regarded with derision by the few people who have seen it. Kate said her favourite poet was John Ashbery.

'Mine too!' I said, even though this is not strictly true (though at that moment it *was* true). '"The truth – that thing I thought I was telling,"' I said. 'I love that line.'

'Where's that from?' said Kate.

'I can't remember,' I lied, not wanting the conversation to become cluttered with footnotes and references. What mattered was that we liked the same things – which, I hoped, was a vicarious way of saying we liked each other. Normally I feel long and skinny as an old branch, but as I sat there in my ULTRA-VIOLENT SKINBLOCK T-shirt, talking about films and poets, I felt tanned and slim and full of the beans I'd had for lunch. Kate had heard I was 'some kind of writer' and wondered what kind of things I wrote.

'I have an idea for a self-help book,' I said. '*Yoga for People Who Can't Be Bothered to Do It.*'

'But you can't be bothered to write it, right?'

'You stole my punch line,' I said.

'Its a good idea, though. Chapter one: "Emptying Your Mind".'

'Oh, I haven't got that far yet.'

'How far have you got?'

'Not far at all. "Near" would be more accurate than "far".'

'So how near have you got?'

'I am near to where I started – but I am even nearer to giving up.'

'How come?'

'My mind is too empty.'

Kate had dried off in the sun, had finished her pad thai, was drinking from a bottle of water. She was a teacher who lived in LA. She worked long hours but was free to take extended vacations. Her life was a combination of the mundane and the glamorous (she used to live with a well-known independent film-maker, she hung out with movie people and attended premieres). She spoke Spanish. She grew up in Philadelphia. Her hair was not any specific colour. At one point she turned in her chair and asked me if her back was peeling. I could see her spine, her spine beneath her skin, which at a certain point disappeared into her bikini. I said no, no it wasn't. She touched her shoulders with her hands.

'Are you sure?' she said, turning this time towards Jake, who confirmed her suspicions that her back was peeling.

'You lied,' she said to me.

'I didn't want to look too closely,' I said coyly.

We continued sitting. No one showed any sign of getting up or leaving until Kate said she was going to her room to take a nap. I wanted to say, 'Me too,' but I couldn't, of course. I watched her gather up her things. She said, 'See you all later,' and the three of us said, 'See you later,' and I avoided watching her walk away. I continued sitting with Jake and Gareth, who also continued sitting. After ten minutes I got up and said, 'See you later,' and left the two of them sitting there. As I walked away I was acutely conscious of the two empty chairs with no one sitting in them.

I saw Kate a couple of hours later when I was on my balcony, hanging out my clothes as I'd been doing for the previous hour and a half, keeping an eye on her balcony. She was wearing her bikini, had just come out on to her balcony.

'Hi!' I called out. 'I didn't know that was your place.'

'Me neither. Know that was yours, I mean.'

'Why don't you come over and visit?' I said.

Within minutes she walked up the steps and on to my balcony. She had a towel around her shoulders and some kind of lotion in her hair.

'I'll have to go back and shower this off,' she said. 'You're meant to wash it out after two minutes.' Three minutes later she was still there, still standing on my balcony.

'You can use my shower,' I said. The words clogged in my throat. She went into the shower, then returned, her hair wet, shiny. I was sitting down in a straightforward, non-yoga way. She was drying her legs with the towel. My face was level with her stomach.

'I've washed it out,' she said, 'but my hair still feels all slippery.' I couldn't stop looking at her breasts and stomach, and after a while I didn't try. It was becoming almost impossible to speak. My heart was thumping so loudly I wanted to take her hand and put it on my chest and say, 'Feel my heart,' but I couldn't do that, couldn't take her hand, and it was this inability to do so that was making my heart beat like crazy. She was running her hand through her hair, which, she said again, felt all slippery. My face was inches from her tummy. If there had been some scientific instrument capable of measuring whatever waves or energy were passing between us, the needles would have gone haywire, back and forth like windscreen wipers. It was like the build-up to a tropical storm, the rumbling of clouds over the mountain separating us from Haad Rin. I could bear it no longer. She moved fractionally towards me and my lips were on her stomach, and then she knelt down and we were kissing, and her hair, wet and slippery, was falling all over me.

*　　*　　*

99

We lay in bed, under my mosquito net, for a long while. As the light faded Kate told me about her grandfather who had been killed on Saipan or wherever, about the letter he wrote, and the town where she grew up. It was dark by the time we showered and went down to dinner. I was, as you can imagine, in very high spirits. I had been at the Sanctuary a week, I had made friends, I felt like I *belonged*, and a couple of hours earlier I'd had sex with Kate. It was already one of the greatest days of my life – and the full-moon party was still to come! You couldn't actually hear it but at some inaudible level you could feel the thump of the music coming over the mountain or around the bay. The atmosphere was the opposite of rowdy; people were reining themselves in, forcing themselves to remain calm, not to get too excited about what lay ahead. Even Troy – whose fucked-up feet meant he wouldn't be going to the party – was relatively sedate, capable of sitting down for minutes on end before getting up and sitting down again. A lot of the talk, naturally, was about drugs – who would take what, in what order, in what quantity, in which combinations, at what time. It was a genre of conversation that Jake felt particularly at home with. Like many people here he had grown into his character – white trash, badass – in the time he had spent at the Sanctuary, and found that it was a character people liked. In his twenties he'd been heavily into drugs, but those days were behind him and now he just drank. Tonight, though, because it was a special occasion, he would make an exception and have a little of whatever he could get his hands on.

'And does that apply to drugs too?' quipped Kate. Confident and fearless she may have been, but she had never taken Ecstasy and was reluctant to do so now. Jake sought to reassure her.

'Ecstasy is a good drug to take on a daily basis,' he explained. This might have flown in the face of all medical and anecdotal evidence, but if the idea was to set her mind at ease, it could not have been more persuasively pitched. Kate, however, was not convinced. I put the matter in starker terms.

'There is only one way to look at it. Do you want to say yes to life? If the answer is yes, then you take E. At least once. If you decide you want to say no to life, then you don't take it.' As I said earlier, it had already been a great day. I was beginning to get very excited about the party and I was, in truth, feeling a bit full of myself. A more convincing argument about taking Ecstasy was being demonstrated by Tammy and John. They were not coming to the party but they were coming up on E. They sat behind Kate, massaging her arms and shoulders, looking like they would happily spend the rest of their life doing nothing else.

'Man,' said Jake, looking at the three of them. 'I am every kind of jealous.'

At midnight two long-tails arrived to take us to the party. The electricity had gone off at the Sanctuary an hour earlier, and the darkness imparted a clandestine character to the operation. The boats rocked and tilted precariously as more and more people clambered aboard. The moon was showing through a gauze of cloud, the water was streaked silver. We pushed away from the shore, silently, nervous in the way you are before these big parties. We waved at John and Tammy, who had come down to the beach to see us off. The noise of the engine, when it was yanked into life, was immense. The palm-fringed beach slipped away. The two boats, ours lit by a red neon tube, the other with a green, powered alongside each other. As the boats pulled out to sea we could see the huge hump of the jungle-covered mountain. We passed Haad Yuan beach. Flying fish skipped through the water. The moon came out from the clouds, a dazzling silver disc. Already some way into a surprisingly strong acid trip, Wayne was sitting next to me, showing signs of going AWOL. He had taken to calling me 'Lieutenant' – as in 'When we hit that beach, Lieutenant . . .' – and kept referring to the boat as a 'landing craft'. Kate was on the other side, her leg pressed next to mine. Occasionally there was a lash of spray from the sea as the boatmen – relaxed, stoned, efficient – steered us towards Haad Rin. The two boats kept close to each other. There was only a slight swell. The sea spanned the horizon. The boats, it seemed, were going as fast as they could, but no one really wanted this trip to end. The sea was dark, sparkling with phosphorescence. The moon blazed overhead, the jungle tumbled down the slopes of the mountain.

As we skirted the last headland we could see Haad Rin, illuminated with fluoro and fires. We could hear the pump of techno above the motor, or rather the motor took on some of the rhythm of the music. Drawing closer we could see the long arc of the beach already crowded with people. Other boats were pouring in, from other beaches on Ko Pha-Ngan, from Ko Samui. The engine slowed to a low chug and the music took over. Rockets were exploding overhead.

'Incoming!' shouted Wayne.

'Man, he is really gone,' said Jake. A moment later so was Jake: he leapt overboard, into deeper water than expected, and disappeared, briefly, beneath the waves. The rest of us disembarked more cautiously and waded to the beach. All around was the pump of sound systems and the blaze of fires and UV. It was mayhem.

We hit the beach and fanned out. We had agreed on a spot we could all come back to at some point in the night in the hope of finding some of the others, but I doubt if anyone remembered where it was. There were a dozen sound systems spread along the beach. From a distance it sounded like techno, but they were actually all playing the same kind of idiotic uplifting trance. We drifted from one sound system to the next, dancing for a bit and then moving on. The party was going off, no doubt about that, but I was never able to lose myself in the music which was really quite idiotic.

At some point Kate and I became separated from everyone else. We spread a sarong on the sand and sat and kissed. I moved my hand beneath her skirt and slipped my fingers inside her. We kissed for ages and my fingers grew so wet it was like oil pouring through them.

'I'm melting,' said Kate. The moon blazed in her eyes, which were the size of mine, reflected in hers, the size of the moon.

By daybreak the beach was devastated. The party was still raging but there were bodies crashed out in the sand. A scum of spent bottles and cigarettes bobbed at the edge of the surf.

While we were waiting for a boat back to the Sanctuary, we met Gareth, who, predictably, had had some bad luck. He

GEOFF DYER

had become confused and spent most of the night wandering round, not finding anyone he knew or anywhere he particularly wanted to be until, finally, he had been taunted by a group of lady boys. Kate put her arm round his shoulders. The boat was already leaving when Jake ran into the surf and hauled himself aboard. Unlike Gareth, but equally predictably, he'd had an amazing time and was only coming back now so he'd be in good shape for the after-party later that day.

'What about Wayne?' he asked. 'Did you see anything of him?'

'When I last saw him, hours ago, he was telling people to "dig in" and calling out for "stretcher bearers".'

'Seriously?'

'Absolutely,' I said. After that we rode in silence, scarcely noticing the clamour of the motor. The sea was glassy, the sky tinged with pink. The world was insubstantial, wonderful, as if it were waking from a dream that was not yet over with.

We got back to the Sanctuary and found Rob sitting at the bar. Some of the others were lying in hammocks, dazed, drifting; others were sleeping; and some – as Rob put it – were 'still unaccounted for'.

Kate came back to my hut. We showered and went to bed as the day grew hot outside.

'How's your mind?' she said.

'Empty,' I said. 'How's yours?'

'Full,' she said.

'Of emptiness?'

'Yes. Exactly.'

There was almost no difference between being awake and being asleep. Sex was like being in the midst of a long pornographic dream from which I awoke to find Kate sleeping next to me, breathing.

The following day both Kate and I were leaving – separately. I was going to Chiang Mai; she was flying to Bangkok, and from there back to California. If it had been the other way round I would have altered my plans and gone with her to Chiang Mai or anywhere else she was going. She was leaving first, on the early boat to Samui. She got up, packed her things, and then came back to my hut to say goodbye. I was awake but still in bed.

'I love your adolescent shoulders,' she said. Then she kissed me on the mouth and was gone.

I left later that morning. Some people were staying, others had already left or were leaving in the next couple of days; but new people were arriving, travellers like me who would arrive not knowing anyone; within a week, though, they would have met people they liked and felt at home with, strangers they became friends with, and – if they were lucky – someone they fell in love with. I was leaving, but I was heading somewhere else, somewhere new, probably to some place the people arriving had just come from.

I paddled into the sea, heaved my rucksack into the long-tail, and climbed aboard. A few minutes later the boat was tugging me away, round the bay towards Haad Rin. There was no wind. The sky was clear, the sea a deep sea blue.

There is something about leaving a place on a small boat – something about the movement of the waves, the noise of the engine: it is like you are leaving your life behind and yet, since you are part of the life you have left behind, part of you is still there. Dying, at its best, might be something like this. Everything was a memory, and everything was still happening in some extended present, and everything was still to come. Earlier that morning, when Kate had come to say goodbye, she had been wearing a dress which – in our subsequent, brief e-mail correspondence – I referred to as gingham.

'Madras,' she wrote back. 'Not gingham. Madras.'

DECLINE AND FALL

In Rome I lived in the grand manner of writers. I basically did nothing all day. Not a thing. Perhaps this is why I was such a seductive role model for many of the aspiring writers who lived near by. More exactly, I was a role model for Nick, the youthful American who lived opposite, who had not read any of my books and to whom my name meant nothing. Nevertheless he knew – from me – that I was a writer, a man who lived by his pen, and we used to chat across the sunless abyss separating his balcony from mine. It was a lovely way to converse about literature and the literary life, such as it is. There we were, two young writers, one unpublished, the other not so young, united by our love of idleness and marijuana. Nick was from California and I wasted no time in letting him know that I was the author of several books, none of which was available from the English bookshop on Via del Moro. He was teaching English in Rome – that was how he earned money – but he was also working on a short story, possibly a series of short stories, linked in some way that was of no interest to me or anyone else.

For my part I was thinking about writing something based around the bit in *Civilization and Its Discontents* where Freud offers the history of Rome as an analogy of 'preservation in the sphere of the mind' (which, I took it, was not quite the same thing as memory). In the actual city, successive phases of building obliterated or obscured all but the 'scanty remains' of earlier architectural achievements. These later buildings in turn became the ruins which are found amid 'the jumble of a great metropolis which has grown up in the last few centuries since the Renaissance'. Freud then asks us to imagine that Rome is not a place but 'a psychical entity with a similarly long and copious past – an entity, that is to say, in which nothing that has once come into existence will have passed away and all the earlier phases of development continue to exist alongside the latest one'. Where the Colosseum now stands, for example, 'we could at the same time admire Nero's vanished Golden House' and anything else that was ever there.

That was the theory, even if I wasn't sure exactly what it meant. In practice it meant that every evening – and most mornings (and some afternoons) – I went to the San Calisto, the best bar in Rome, probably Italy, possibly the world. The Calisto was such a fixture of life in Trastevere that it was hard to imagine a time when it – or its clientele – had not been there. Restaurants and resorts often boast of their 'exclusive' status, but most of the world's best places are the opposite of exclusive – and nowhere was less exclusive than the Calisto. The Calisto made a prison look exclusive. It wasn't just that everyone was welcome; everyone was actually *there*. Heroin addicts, film directors, journalists, models, garbage collectors, tourists, drunks, nutters, doctors, waiters from other bars that had already closed – they all ended up at the Calisto. Some started out there as well. There was no need ever to arrange to meet anyone at the San Calisto: you simply assumed they would be there. Most of my friends went to the San Calisto; some of them I saw only at the San Calisto. On busy nights – from June to the middle of August and from late August to the middle of October – it was impossible to tell where the Calisto terrace ended and the nearby piazza began. Parked mopeds became chairs, cars became tables. It was as hot at one in the morning as it is in England at one in the afternoon in the middle of a heat wave. No wonder the air was heavy with desire. It might not have been enshrined in the constitution, but women's right to bare arms was everywhere in evidence. As I talked to her (about the heat) I calculated that, aside from sandals, Nick's flirtatious friend Monica was wearing just two items of clothing. I could see only one of these – her dress, sleeveless, light blue – and was very curious about what the other looked like.

'I know what you are thinking,' she said.

'What?' I said.

'You are thinking about my underwear.'

'How did you know that?'

'It is obvious.'

'What am I thinking about them?'

'You are thinking that they are white.'

'Correct.'

'That they are made of cotton.'

'Also correct.'

'That they are very small.'

'Yes, exactly,' I said. 'Am I right?'

Instead of answering, Monica slipped off her moped and slinked into the bar, leaving me with a tightness in my chest so intense I felt I might cave in. If the conversation had gone on a little longer I would have told Monica about the film I wanted to make, a film with her in it. In my head I could see this film very clearly. It consisted of white columns against a blue sky ('as blue as the most exploded tradition'), filmed at Hadrian's Villa and – late in the day, with blazing yellow walls and looming shadows – on Via della Luce. It would have some of the qualities of De Chirico and the spatial emptiness of Antonioni, and Monica would wander through it like a Hope Sandoval song. I was going to call it *The Meaning of Antiquity*, and a month earlier I had bought a second-hand super-8 camera to begin shooting it.

Since buying it I had taken the camera out of its sturdy leather case only once (to fiddle with the focus and zoom) and had no intention of doing so again. I didn't even buy any film. The instructions were complicated and I knew there would be a frustrating shortfall between the majesty of my cinematic conception and the technical means of realizing it. I also had a superstitious belief that if I learned how to use that camera and made a movie, then I would be even more finished as a writer than I already was. I could have combined things and written a script, but my idea of movie-making, I explained to Nick (who also liked the idea of making films), precluded the idea of working from a script. It also precluded the idea of making a movie, but this did not stop Nick and me hanging out at the San Calisto and talking as though we were two cinéastes with distinguished bodies of work already behind us and several projects in preproduction.

'The long takes,' I said, 'the way that silence becomes a

form of dialogue, almost a character in its own right – that was such a feature in your early work, but recently you seem to have moved towards a faster, more *audible* visual style.'

'I think that's right,' said Nick. 'The silence is still there, but I wanted people to look harder to find it, to hear it.'

'You know what I'd like to do? Get right back to basics. Get away from production values. No actors, no script. Just shoot some footage. You know, just me and the camera—'

'Film—'

'Exactly,' I said. We clinked glasses, united by the purity of our idea of cinema.

Although I never took it out of its case or bought any film, I often wished I had my super-8 camera with me because I saw movies everywhere in Rome. There were no films worth seeing at the cinemas – any that were worth seeing were dubbed into Italian and thereby rendered not worth seeing – but the streets were full of films. On Via del Corso a marching band and majorette parade brought traffic to a standstill; at some point the parade even brought itself to a temporary standstill, but the band, as they say, played on. The girls did their majorette routine, kicking up their legs with an enthusiasm that more than compensated for any lack of synchronization. One majorette was particularly gorgeous and I watched a young fellow watch her intently. His eyes never left her. All the time he was eating a pink gelato. It was boiling hot. The ice cream dripped as he licked it. She continued dancing, he tongued his dripping gelato. It was unbelievably lascivious but, at the same time, the guy was so deadpan – and she ignored him so studiously – that he was, to all intents and purposes, *just eating an ice cream*. It was superb: part of the spontaneous choreography of Roman life that was also like a scene from a film. The name of this film? *Being Roman.*

Romans spend their lives auditioning for roles in this long-running tragi-comedy. Take, for example, the young woman – seventeen at most – who was caught riding her Vespa the wrong way up Via Arenula. Everyone else was doing the same thing, but she was the one who got pulled over by a *vigile*. He was wearing an impeccably ironed blue shirt, motorbike boots and aviator shades in which she could see her reflection ricocheting off the sunglasses of all the observing extras who were standing round watching. She was wearing a yellow sundress. Her legs and arms were bare, tanned. The *vigile* asked to see her papers, which were not in order. Double jeopardy! She begged forgiveness. He refused to relent. It was a man-woman thing, a uniform-dress thing. He was going to punish her for her transgression. At first she pleaded, then she flirted, then she started crying. They may have been crocodile tears but they were real as well: real crocodile tears. Eventually he let her off. Why? Partly because it's a Catholic country (forgiveness! redemption!), but mainly because she had played her part so well (which, in turn, allowed him to play his part well). She had passed the audition. They had both starred in the ongoing movie of Rome.

Another time, out riding around Testaccio, I came across an accident. A Vespa was sprawled out in the road. The road sparkled with broken glass. A crowd had gathered round a young woman who lay near by, covered in a blanket. There was some blood on the road. It was awful – but it was only a film. A real film, I mean, one with cameras, lights and crew. After a while the victim got up and they staged the whole thing over again. I was relieved that it wasn't real, that the accident hadn't really happened, because collision, injury and death were very real possibilities. Romans claim that riding scooters isn't at all dangerous, but the city is full of the halt and the lame, limpers with legs in plaster and arms in slings. One morning the woman who ran the *tabaccheria* next door to where I lived turned up with a black eye, a graze down one side of her face, and a thick bandage on one arm.

'What happened?' I asked.

'*Motorino*,' she said in the resigned tone of one who accepts injury and suffering as facts of life. The roads were cobbled, slippery, prone to subsidence, and a moment's lapse of concentration amid the gladiatorial traffic could be fatal. I often spent the afternoons driving round on my moped and I was always relieved when I made it back home in one piece. If Nanni Moretti had not already done so I would have made a film of these terrifying, exhilarating journeys through the *quartieri* of Rome with the Köln Concert on the soundtrack. You never knew what you were going to see in Rome, but you always saw something, even if it was just three men loading a four-seater sofa on to the roof rack of a Cinquecento or – 'What a nice surprise!' – Monica on her Vespa, waiting at traffic lights on Lungotevere. I was on foot, just idling; she was on her way to Disfu, the record store over in San Lorenzo. Did I want to come with her, for the ride?

'Sure,' I said.

'Hop on,' she said. Because Monica was Roman she drove much faster than I ever dared, and the city veered past in a series of terrifying near misses. We were not wearing helmets, of course. I sat tightly behind her and held on to her waist.

I did not move my hands up towards her breasts. I kept them resting on her hipbones, which I could feel, quite clearly, through her skin and through her dress.

Other than risking injury, defying death and tempting fate on the moped, and hanging out at the San Calisto, I did very little. One night I went with Nick to an open-air screening of De Sica's *Bicycle Thieves*. Neither of us had seen this masterpiece of neo-realism before, and it came as a major disappointment to both of us.

'If it was meant to be so realistic, why didn't he just lock up his bike?' said Nick in the Calisto afterwards.

In the morning I crossed Ponte Sisto to buy cherry tomatoes and cherry-flavoured cherries at Campo dei Fiori, where, periodically, I also bought a magazine. In the middle of the square the cowled statue of Giordano Bruno – burned at the stake for adhering to the theories of Copernicus – stood brooding in the tall heat. The Latin inscription included the word *arse*. Extrapolating from this, I assumed that the inscription as a whole explained that this was where Bruno got his arse burned. After lunch, when the stalls had packed up and the trampled detritus of the market had been carted away, Campo dei Fiori was devastated, empty; but at night it became as crowded as Bombay – not quite as crowded as Bombay, obviously, but as crowded as the San Calisto certainly, as crowded as everywhere else in Rome.

And then, gradually, as July turned to August, the city began to thin out. Places started shutting; where previously there was a display of groceries, now there was only a graffitied metal shutter and a sticker announcing that the shop had closed for holidays. Each day another shop, another restaurant, another market stall closed. Each day another friend went on holiday. I spent whole afternoons saying goodbye, meeting people for coffee at the Calisto before they left the city, putting a brave face on my lack of travel plans ('Somebody's got to steer the ship,' I said). Apart from Nick, everyone I knew was going away. Each day the city became hotter, emptier, quieter. The streets succumbed to a kind of eclipse: they looked, in bright daylight, as they did at night when all the shutters were down. 'Noon-time's stupor' began to last all day, all week. It was August, 'the month of stalled pendulums', and I too was stalled, staying put.

Tourists continued to arrive but they weren't really an occupying force. Their itineraries were busy, they were on the move constantly, and they flocked principally to places frequented by pigeons: Saint Peter's, the Spanish Steps, Piazza Navona, and the Campidoglio, where a German couple asked Nick to take their picture as they stood stoically in front of Marcus Aurelius and his horse. He obliged, automatically, and they thanked him with an outpouring of gratitude that seemed excessive in the era of point and click. Or maybe that was just the acid coming on. Did I neglect to mention that we had dropped a couple of microdots an hour and a half previously? Well, if I did, we had. It was part of my investigations into the research potential of what I liked to call acid archae-ology, or *pyschedelica antiqua*: using LSD to scrape away the intervening years and achieve unmediated access to the living past. Either that or it was just a way of whiling away the week-long days. Like many Californians Nick was a very relaxing person to trip with. It wasn't the white-knuckle ride that it so often was for me, and if I wanted to see it as 'a psychoactive equivalent of what Piranesi did in his etchings', that was cool with him. Although the lips of his statue did not move, we assumed that it was Marcus Aurelius – not his horse – who said, 'All the blessings which you pray to obtain hereafter could be yours today, if you did not deny them to yourself.' The Roman legionnaires – three of them – were neither real nor hallucinatory, merely props for tourists' photos, and they smoked between shots.

The people drifting through the remnants of the Forum – we went there after the Campidoglio – were not the ghosts of contemporaries of Trajan or Nero but of all those eighteenth-century tourists, looking up at the Arch of Titus, aghast at the grandeur of antiquity. The Colosseum was an antique roundabout made of Tom and Jerry cheese – or from a distance it was, anyway. Inside, it was good to feel the stones of the Colosseum breathe, to know that quarried rock has its life too. The exhaust-smeared stones pulsed and rippled with life, warm and vital as a stroked animal. For a few minutes anything seemed possible. I was within reach of the stillness at the centre of the stone, the place where prayer originates or ends up. The prayer, of course, is always the same: let me be rid of time, as indifferent to its passing as the sleeping stone. It's a prayer answered, in part, by the lithe figures of classical antiquity: motionless, embalmed in stone, living on in a time that has died.

That must be why we went back to the Campidoglio to see the fragmented remains of Constantine: his head, a swollen bicep, the right hand pointing skywards, a foot – all sooty white, each bigger than a person. It was hard to imagine these bits and pieces joined together in a single gleaming body, even harder to believe that they had been carved by human hands; it seemed more likely that they had come into existence through a process or upheaval akin to those which form glaciers and mountains. Someone was sitting by these gigantic fragments, head in hands, overwhelmed, apparently, by the grandeur of antiquity. It took a while to realize that it was me sitting there. I wasn't just overwhelmed: I wanted to enter the dead time of statues and see things through their unpupiled eyes, from their point of view (day strobing into night, centuries flickering past in hours); I was in no hurry (it was still only three o'clock), and besides, I had nothing else to do. It may well have happened, if only for a moment. Nick took a photo of me sitting there, overwhelmed by antiquity, and when the pictures came back I was quite difficult to see: fading, ghostly transparent, impermanent.

More and more places closed, but the San Calisto remained open – thank God. I sat outside with a dozen other humans, a couple of cats and a dog of uncertain ownership, crammed into a ledge of shadow, feeling left behind. One of the humans was Nick. We talked about the old days, our œuvre, shots and angles, interminable pans, the belated influence of neo-realism on his work and of *The Italian Job* on mine. I thought of *The Meaning of Antiquity*, the film I had not shot, specifically the Hadrian's Villa sequence. Four of us – Nick, me, Monica and a friend of Monica's called Christina – had driven out to Tivoli in Christina's car, leaving Rome on a curving autostrada that reminded me of San Francisco, the view from highway 101. We drifted round the huge site. No one had a map and we did not know exactly what we were seeing: statues lifeguarding pools of green water reflecting white pillars against a green-blue sky, a headless statue, a stone crocodile sunbathing, the sound of crickets.

At one point Monica and I found ourselves alone in the scanty remains of the Temple of Venus. It was difficult to believe that what was here had ever been intended to enclose, to hide from view, to create an interior; it seemed, instead, that the purpose of the temple was to draw attention to what it revealed, to frame the landscape that sizzled into the distance. We ate some of the figs we had bought in Rome at Campo dei Fiori. Monica was wearing a fun T-shirt – I DO BAD THINGS – and cargo pants. Between the two I could see her tanned stomach, a silver ring glinting in her navel. Her hair was shadow dark and I was watching her eat a fig. I was eating one too. I was acutely conscious, obviously, of the Lawrence poem and the scene in the film of *Women in Love* where Alan Bates, who plays Birkin, quotes the poem. The experience came dripping in quotation marks. Monica was eating a fig with her full mouth, filling her mouth with fig.

'How is your fig?' she said.

I said it was the sweetest fig I had ever tasted.

'Is it wet?' said Monica.

'Yes, very.'

'And is it juicy?'

'It is wet with juice,' I said. She licked her fingers, licked the juice off her fingers. I did the same with mine and wiped them on my shorts. The sky made two thousand years ago seem like yesterday, and yesterday looked like today, just as today would, in time, look like tomorrow. Framed against the sky were white columns, crenellated, broken. A single cloud had drifted to a standstill. The air was abuzz with bees but there was no wind and the trees were quite still. We both felt the spell of antiquity, its clarity and force. That must be why, a few minutes later, Monica said, 'I was born in Libya.'

'Were you?' I said.

'Yes,' she said. 'In Tripoli. I must show you pictures. I have photos of the Roman ruins there.'

'I'd like to see them,' I said.

Such event-packed days were soon no more than a memory; perhaps they were not even a memory, more like a dream. There was less and less to do, which was just as well because I had less and less energy to do anything. It became more and more difficult to accomplish anything, which was just as well because there was nothing to accomplish. I had never before realized how vast a day could be. I was very conscious of living alone, of the way that in the morning everything was exactly where I had left it the night before. The phone was broken; either that or it had lost interest in ringing. From time to time I dialled a digit or two – not to make a call, simply to check that it was working. Air-conditioning would have helped, but it was too late for that now. At this time I was becoming interested in Frank O'Hara's 'I do this I do that' poems and briefly considered founding a counter-movement along the lines of 'I did not do this and I did not do that' but, predictably, I did not do this. So what *did* I do? I *dreamed* a great deal, dreams of a tumble-dry bright-ness I'd never experienced before. It was because of the light, I think. The sky was so bright that the Goncourts, when they were here in 1867, became nostalgic for grey. During the day my eyes and head filled up with a quantity of brightness that my brain couldn't digest, and so it worked overtime, while I was asleep, concocting hours of deranged and brilliant footage as a way of using up the wash and surge of surplus colour and excess light. That was one explanation and I had no need of another.

'I used to want to film my dreams,' I said to Nick. 'Now I'm content to dream my films.'

'You think dreams are better than films?' asked Nick.

'Yes,' I said. 'You know why?'

'It doesn't make any difference if you sleep right through them?'

'Um, that's right,' I said.

'That knocked the wind out of your sails, didn't it?' said Nick.

'Had there been any wind around it would have done, yes.'

The heat was African, still, dead. Like soil parched by years of drought, the sky had had all the life scorched from it. There were no clouds, obviously, and it was unlikely that any would dare come within a hundred miles of anywhere near here. The sun didn't budge. I looked forward to those moments – two or three a day – when a little breeze sneaked into the apartment for a breather. Otherwise the only way to get things moving was by going out on the moped, cruising the sun-stunned city, hoping to run into Monica. I rode up to the Janiculum and looked down at the city, its baked roofs, the Jerusalem dryness of everything. It was very quiet up there. The crickets had packed up and gone on vacation. The days passed even though it didn't feel like they did. I say this with some confidence because eventually it was Ferragosto, the fifteenth of August, and everything of the almost nothing that had remained open closed. It was the opposite of an earthquake. Nothing moved and there was nothing to do. Absolutely nothing. Everything stopped. Even time. There was no traffic and there were no shops and there were no people and there was no time. There was just me and the epic sun which showed no sign of going anywhere. I couldn't buy anything and, as a result, was filled with terrible cravings – for friends, for cherries, for pizzas, for all the things I'd failed to lay in against this siege of sun and motionlessness. Everyone had gone away. Even Nick. Monica was nowhere to be seen. Everyone was nowhere to be seen. Except me. If there had been anyone to do the seeing, I was there for all to see.

Accompanied by a lone crisp packet I crossed Lungotevere without even glancing at the traffic light. From the Ponte Sisto I saw that the Tiber itself was no longer flowing. Nothing moved except the shadows, most of which were indoors anyway. I passed through Piazza Farnese to Campo dei Fiori and Corso Vittorio Emanuele. The lack of traffic meant that I was seized with a desire to get in a car and drive somewhere. But where? The only place I really wanted to go was Rome, and I was there already. I walked in the direction of the Campidoglio and the Forum, pulverized by the sun, entertaining implausible doubts as to my own existence: *If a tree falls in the forest and there's no one around to see or hear it, has it indeed fallen?* – that kind of thing. In my heart of hearts, though, I had no doubts on that score and dozens about everything else. I headed for the Campidoglio and it was there, as I sat musing amid the ruins of the Capitol, that the idea of writing a book about antiquity came to seem an impossible undertaking. It did not manifest itself immediately, definitively, but I had a premonition that any hopes I had once entertained of writing such a book would one day lie in ruins about me. I had been drifting for years, and now – like the lone cloud we'd seen at Hadrian's Villa – I had drifted to a standstill. I may not have admitted it at the time – if that afternoon was a turning point, then I responded as one invariably does at such moments, by failing to turn – but at some level I knew that I had been kidding myself: that all the intellectual discipline and ambition of my earlier years had been dissipated by half-hearted drug abuse, indolence and disappointment, that I lacked purpose and direction and had even less idea of what I wanted from life now than I had when I was twenty or thirty even, that I was well on the way to becoming a ruin myself, and that that was fine by me.

THE DESPAIR OF
ART DECO

The only time I have ever seen a dead body was in South Beach, in the heart of the Art Deco district. It is possible that seeing a dead body there has had an undue influence on my view of Art Deco; but it is also possible that Art Deco has had an undue influence on my view of the dead body. The two are related, I think.

We flew to Miami from boring Nassau and got a bus to South Beach. It was a Sunday, the sidewalks were crammed with visitors, but finding a hotel was not difficult because it was a Sunday and visitors who had come for the weekend had already checked out of their hotels. We checked in at the Beachcomber, a nice-looking place on Collins in the heart of the Art Deco area. That is a pretty meaningless remark, I know. Art Deco, after all, means nice looking, or, more exactly, not as nice as it looks. Our room at the Beachcomber, for example, did not look quite as nice as the façade of the Beachcomber but it still looked pretty nice. An Art Deco lamp shade bathed the Art Deco sheets in an amber Art Deco glow. When we drew back the curtains the Art Deco spell was broken. The window was cracked, grimy, and the surge of dusty sunlight revealed a damp patch spreading across the carpet from the bathroom wall almost to the centre of the room. Then a mouse raced across the marshy carpet and squeezed, with difficulty, under the skirting board of the cramped and mouldy bathroom. Dazed stood on a chair and, with no trace of emotion, said, 'Eek! A mouse!'

'I'll deal with it,' I said.

'You mean you'll try to get a discount on the room?'

'Exactly.'

I went out to the pony-tailed fellow at reception and asked if we could change rooms because there was a mouse in our room, in the room we were in at the moment, and we would prefer a room without a mouse or, if no other room was available—

'Welcome to the tropics,' he said. He didn't shrug. There was no need. His voice shrugged. As it happens, we had just *come* from the tropics, where we had not seen a single mouse, and so I said, 'This is not the tropics.' Although the mouse was not a problem for me, I went on, my girlfriend was 'freaked out by it'.

'Freaked out?'

'Yes, freaked. As in "Eek!"'

'Whatever,' he said, handing me a key to a room on the first floor. 'Take a look at that one.'

It was nice, I said when I went back down, but it was not made up. Next he offered to upgrade us to a larger room, room 15, if I remember rightly. That was nice too, but somebody had been smoking in there, I explained, and it smelt smoky.

'Try 13,' he said, handing me another key. I was beginning to wonder if any rooms were occupied. As it happens,

13 *was* – by a woman, French, I think, sitting on the toilet. This really baffled him. According to his computer, room 13 was definitely empty, but he suggested I try 6. Six was empty, mouseless, smokeless, made up, unoccupied, actually nicer than where we were. An upgrade was as good as a discount. Fine, I said. In the meantime he had sent someone up to 13 and there was no one there.

'You must have gone to the wrong room,' he said.

'Then how could I have opened the door?' I shot back.

'Some keys work for more than one room.'

'Ah.' As soon as we had moved our stuff into 6 we went out for a walk, to buy smoothies, to experience the Art Deco experience for ourselves. Although we had just booked into an Art Deco hotel, we kept stopping off at other Art Deco hotels to see if we would have been better off in another Art Deco hotel. We compared prices and quality ('The price-quality axis, as it were,' I said). There were several other hotels we could have stayed in but, overall, we had quite a good deal.

'We could have got a better deal,' I summarized. 'But we don't have the worst possible deal. Obviously, we could have paid more and stayed at a better place.'

'Or paid less and stayed at a worse place.'

'But we haven't found a place that was more expensive *and* worse.'

'And is that really what we're looking for?'

'In a sense, yes. For peace of mind.'

'But there is always the chance that in looking for a place that is more expensive and worse we might find a place that is better and cheaper.'

'Thereby destroying any chance of ever achieving peace of mind.'

'Perhaps we shouldn't look at any more hotels, then.'

Except that's what you come to South Beach for: to see hotels. The hotels – the Art Deco hotels – are the attraction. Effectively, the Art Deco experience is the hotel experience. Staying in hotels is a side-effect of wanting to see them. In a place with so many hotels, it is the residents who are the tourists, who are not at home. So we continued to look at hotels but we refrained from enquiring about vacancies and rates. Except at the Mermaid Guest House, which was a little more expensive than the Beachcomber but infinitely lovelier. Much of the Art Deco architecture in South Beach is actually a derivative or variant of Art Deco known as Tropical Deco; the Mermaid takes this tendency a little further, away from Deco towards Tropical. We both wished we were staying there – having come from the mouseless tropics, it would have lent a continuity to our trip – but since we had already booked into the Beachcomber there was, Dazed said, no use crying over spilled milk.

After the Mermaid we didn't ask about vacancies and rates at any other hotels. We didn't enquire at the Victor on Ocean Drive because this vast, gleaming white building was unoccupied: utterly vacant, a site of abandoned meaning, in fact, unless the provision of accommodation is considered a side-effect of the Art Deco effect, in which case it was a site of purified meaning. With windows boarded up and painted over, it looked, Dazed said, 'like Rachel Whiteread's Art Deco sequel to *House*'.

A little further on, still on Ocean Drive, a guy with

drive-by shades asked Dazed where she'd got her hair braided. Dazed told him Cat Island. He was asking, really, on behalf of his girlfriend, who was blonde and Russian. He was black and Cuban. They were a very modern couple but they were the product also of a long-standing political alliance. They asked us to take their picture in front of the house – mansion, actually – we were standing in front of.

'You know what house this is?' the Cuban said.

'No.'

'Versace's house,' he said. 'This is where he was gunned down.'

Dazed handed their camera back and they walked off. I studied the bloodless sidewalk. Dazed said, 'This is where he was gunned down.'

'Yes,' I said. 'This is where he was gunned down.'

'Do you remember what you were doing on the night he was gunned down?'

'People are always getting gunned down,' I said. 'No. What were you doing?'

'When?'

'On the night he was gunned down.'

'Who?'

'Specifically, Versace, but anyone really. Anyone who was gunned down.'

'Malcolm X was gunned down, wasn't he, darling?'

'Yes, although he wasn't nearly so well known as a fashion designer.'

'But those glasses he wore have become very fashionable. You see lots of people wearing them. You have a pair, don't you, darling?'

'Yes. And you know the really weird thing?'

'What?'

'They are made by Versace.'

'That is so creepy.'

While we were having this conversation quite a few people were photographed on the spot where Versace was gunned down. I was one of them: Dazed took a picture of me with the disposable camera we had bought in Nassau. Until we had done this we found it difficult to tear ourselves away from the spot, the spot where people were having their pictures taken, the spot where Versace had been gunned down.

It was time, Dazed suggested, to refresh ourselves with a smoothie. We sucked our smoothies – mine had a protein supplement – sitting on a wall by the beach, and I made notes for an essay on Art Deco.

'It is not accurate,' I wrote,

> to say that a shabbiness lurks behind the façade of Art Deco: Art Deco is the façade. Art Deco is the most visible of architectural styles, arranged entirely for the eye – it's in colour! – rather than to be inhabited. Art Deco buildings are inhabited, of course, but whereas, from the outside, they look extraordinary, inside, the experience is fairly ordinary. But this is why the Art Deco style is so alluring.
>
> The block of flats where I have lived in Brixton, London, since the early eighties is, essentially, a utilitarian, age-of-austerity version of Art Deco, without the trappings of Art Deco – without the things that make it Art Deco. These could be added with next to

no effort and at minimal expense, and the building
could be transformed into an Art Deco block, whereupon
this area of flats would become as pleasing to the eye as
South Beach. The flats themselves would remain the same
– but how lovely it would be to feel that we lived in the
Art Deco area of Brixton rather than in a shabby block
of flats. We could even call it South Beach, Brixton.

Twilight was falling. The sand dulled. We began walking back to our hotel. Pale in the afternoon sunlight, neon – purple, glowing, green – was coming into its own. The sky grew ink dark.

Back at the Beachcomber it turned out that we were not the only ones to have changed rooms. The mouse had come too. It was in the wastepaper basket, eating dinner. We preferred to think that it was the same mouse because that was preferable, I said, to admitting that the hotel was actually 'a vermin-infested rat hole'.

'You can't call it a rat hole,' said Dazed.

'Why not?'

'Because a mouse is not a rat.'

'But a mouse is a vermin, isn't it?'

'I don't know what a vermin is.'

'Mice and rats are vermin.'

'Are you a vermin, darling?'

'And since rats and mice are vermin, a mouse is, in a sense, a species of rat.'

'Am *I* a vermin, darling?'

'So, logically, it is quite accurate to call a place infested with mice a rat hole.'

'It is a rat hole, isn't it, darling?'

That night I woke up several times, hearing rustling and scurrying. In the morning there were mouse droppings on the spare bed and the mouse had chewed through Dazed's make-up bag.

'Look,' she said, holding up a copy of our slightly nibbled guide to the Bahamas. 'It chewed off more than it could bite.'

'D'you think it might eat my computer?' I said.

'I'm worried that it might eat *us*.'

Before going out we stashed our belongings away on high shelves in the wardrobe, out of harm's way, so it would be harder for the mouse to eat them.

'The mouse is terrorizing us, isn't it?' said Dazed as we locked our room with a key that, in all probability, opened other rooms as well.

'It really is.'

'It's gnawing away at our self-esteem.'

By the time we had breakfast it was already hot as anything. The sky was a sharp blue. I had a seven-dollar haircut from a Cuban barber who sang while he worked, paying almost no attention to the job – cutting my hair – in hand. At a space-conditioned bookstore on Lincoln, Dazed bought a book, *Miami* by Joan Didion, which seemed a very sensible choice. The sun ricocheted off the walls and sidewalk. Even though neither of us is interested in cars, there were lots of interesting cars to look at. Without any warning Dazed asked what I would do if she threw herself in front of one of these cars. I said I didn't know, but my general policy is not to get involved. We went into record stores and clothes stores and picked up flyers for trance parties that had taken place the day before we arrived. Every clothes store played trance but we didn't find any clothes we wanted or any parties we could go to. We just walked around really, looking at hotels and flyers, buying smoothies, living the Art Deco life. Then a hustler with wayward hair and unkempt eyes accosted us.

'D'you speak English?' he wanted to know.

'To a very high standard,' I said.

'Could you do me a favour?'

'Almost certainly not,' I said. For a moment he looked totally crestfallen. Then he went on his way without even saying, 'Fuck you.' In its way it was one of the most satisfying exchanges of my life. He could have been the risen Christ for all we cared.

What else? We watched some beach volleyball and then Dazed borrowed a guy's blades – her feet are quite big – and bladed for a while. She didn't even ask. He offered. I sat talking to him, just stuff to say while he swigged fat-free milk from a carton and we both watched Dazed gliding and turning on his blades. After blading she wanted to go back to the hotel because it was so hot and the heat was getting to her. I walked with her back to the Beachcomber, and then strolled on regardless.

In the course of my stroll I became convinced that the Gap, on Collins, was designed to look like an Art Deco whale, some kind of fish anyway. One window served as an eye, three more as teeth. It even had fins and gills. I stared at it for a while, unsure if this was just the heat talking. Speaking of talking, I wished Dazed had been there so we could have had one of our so-called conversations about the whale, about whether it was a fish or not.

Further on, one side of the street was cordoned off with black-and-yellow film: POLICE LINE DO NOT CROSS. A crowd, of which I was a part, gathered. Something had happened. You could tell something had happened by the way we were all standing round asking what had happened. There was an ambulance, several police cars. A photographer was taking photographs, standing over . . . the body! I say body but I could see only the feet of the body, the grubby white socks. The rest of the body was hidden from view by bushes.

'What happened?' I said to the guy next to me. He had a tattoo of a washing machine on his arm.

'Suicide.'

'Oh my.'

'A seventy-two-year-old woman. She jumped.'

'Shit. Hey, I like the tattoo, by the way.'

'Thanks.'

'Is it any particular kind of washing machine?'

'Oh it's, like, just a general model, I guess.'

'What floor did she jump from?'

'Fourteenth.'

'So, roughly speaking, that would be between the thirteenth and the fifteenth, right?' I said. I began counting from the ground floor up but soon lost track. The situation was made more complex by the way that, in America, the first floor is actually the ground floor and the second is the first and so on. The fourteenth was about two-thirds of the way up.

'Happens all the time,' the guy with the tattoo of a washing machine on his arm said.

'Does it?'

'It's the heat.'

'What?'

'Drives people nuts.'

'What does?'

'The heat.'

'Yes,' I said, 'I can imagine,' but I was also thinking that Rome is just as hot as Miami and people don't throw themselves off fourteenth-floor balconies there.

'Drives people nuts,' he repeated.

'Perhaps Art Deco generates a kind of despair,' I said. 'Is that possible?'

'Anything's possible,' he said. Across the road the photographer was taking photographs of the body. In fact the whole scene looked like one of those staged photographs of the dead by Nick Waplington. I had never seen a dead body before, and now I was seeing one. Or seeing a pair of socks anyway. I was not sure that counted. To really see a dead body perhaps you have to see the mashed head, the bloody face, but all I could see was the grubby white socks of the dead woman, whose body would soon be zipped up in a body bag.

Back at the hotel Dazed was asleep on the bed and had not been eaten by the mouse, which, I had to concede, was actually the mice, several of whom scurried away when I entered the room. I took a shower in the shabby bathroom and then told Dazed about the dead woman. She was very sympathetic, reassuring me that although I had seen only her socks, it still counted: I could say that I had seen a dead body.

That evening we ate in the same restaurant we had eaten in the night before. In the morning I took Dazed to the spot, the spot where the woman had jumped. Something about

South Beach urges you to do this, to visit spots where people have been gunned down or have thrown themselves off balconies.

'It's a place,' Dazed said, 'with a remarkable capacity to generate sites of instant pilgrimage.' I could see now that the old lady had been extremely considerate, jumping into a recess, set back slightly from the sidewalk, so that she would not land on anyone. There was no stain or anything, no dent. Dazed took a picture of me but I was a little nervous standing there in case someone else came down on top of me.

'Hurry up,' I said.

'Why?'

'This is a part of the world where people fall through the air at speed,' I said. After Dazed had taken the picture we crossed the road and I saw that the balconies on one side of the building were all empty except for chairs on which no one sat. Dazed said that the building was flying at half-mast and I understood what she meant.

We looked at more hotels, enjoyed some more smoothies. Later in the day I saw an old woman hobbling along through the swarming, tanned bodies of the fit and young, the stoned trancers and tattooed bladers, the gay men all pumped up with protein supplements and power boosts, the pierced, slim, salad-eating women for whom Art Deco was an incentive to display and not a source of shoddy despair that could drive you to suicide. I admired the old woman's tenacity, the way she kept going, kept putting one arthritic foot in front of another. As she passed by she lurched suddenly forward – one of her knees must have given way – and almost fell over. She smiled at me when she had regained her balance and I realized that it was the same woman I had seen yesterday, lying on the sidewalk. I was glad that she had made such a speedy recovery. I knew it was her because of her socks, which were grubby, white, unbloodied.

HOTEL OBLIVION

Although Dave was English and lived in Milan, we – Dazed and I – called him Amsterdam Dave because that's where we met him, in Amsterdam. We were there for the fortieth birthday of our friend Matt. Matt doesn't live in Amsterdam either but his wife, Alexandra, had booked them into a suite at the 717 on Prinsengracht for the weekend. She had also invited a dozen of Matt's friends to spend the weekend in Amsterdam. Obviously Alexandra was not going to spring for everyone's accommodation; the deal was that on Friday she and Matt would take us all out to dinner, and then on Saturday they would receive us in their lavish suite for drinks: a kind of 'at home' away from home. Matt's more successful friends booked themselves rooms at the 717, but Dazed and I checked into a cheap hotel inconveniently located some way from the centre of town. As it happened, Amsterdam Dave was staying there as well, but much more important than this administrative coincidence was our shared sense of the obligations imposed on us by a weekend in Amsterdam. Nearly everyone in our party liked the idea of dinner followed by a few joints in a bar, but only Amsterdam Dave was committed to making it a truly memorable weekend in the sense that he would remember nothing whatsoever about it. I was in the twilight, the long autumn of my psychedelic years, and this was to be my last hurrah – or one of them, at any rate. I had never met Amsterdam Dave before but I took to him from the moment he explained the philosophical basis of the weekend.

'It's all about moderation,' he said in the Greenhouse on Friday night, after a deliciously inauthentic Thai meal. 'Everything in moderation. Even moderation itself. From this it follows that you must, from time to time, have excess. And this is going to be one of those occasions.'

'I couldn't agree more,' I said, impressed by the rigour of his thinking. 'As I see it we are here to do the Dam. We want to have the Amsterdam experience.'

'Indeed we do,' said Amsterdam Dave. On Saturday morning, accordingly, we made our way to the Magic Mushroom Gallery on Spuistraat. Amsterdam Dave looked slightly the worse for wear; that is to say, he looked in better shape than he would for the rest of the weekend. This was partly because he had stayed on at a club called the Trance Buddha or Buddha Trance or something long after we had turned in, but mainly it was because Amsterdam Dave never looked better than slightly the worse for wear. I have seen him on several occasions since that weekend in Amsterdam and I have never seen him look anything like as good as he did then. His face had some colour in it. That colour was grey, admittedly, but at least it was a colour. Other times, only his eyes and the hair at his temples were grey; the last vestige of colour had been completely drained from the rest of his face. Even his lips were pale. But that October morning in Amsterdam he looked great, relatively speaking.

Dazed looked lovely too, unequivocally so. She was wearing a woolly hat that I had bought her as an advance Christmas present, and this, combined with her wonky tortoiseshell glasses, gave her the appearance of an eccentric intellectual beauty, a nutty archaeologist, say, as played by a Hollywood actress who was in her thirties and trying not to rely solely on her looks, determined to show that she could do character. And me? Oh, doubtless I looked a complete joke. From the outside you would have thought I was the kind of person whose overyouthful wardrobe – skateboarding T-shirt, trainers, hooded sweatshirt – could not disguise the fact that he was forty-two, an intellectual with nothing but ink to his name; but for much of that weekend, I felt myself to be at the height of my powers – or thereabouts. I concede that we may have looked an oddly matched trio as we sat down in a café to consume our newly purchased mushrooms, but I was not expecting to get thrown out quite as soon as we did. Not thrown out exactly, but given a very stern talking-to by the barman. He didn't want us doing mushrooms in here, he said. This took a moment to sink in: we were being ejected from a bar in Amsterdam for taking drugs?

'That's like getting chucked out of a pub for drinking beer,' said Dazed. I have achieved very little in my life – perhaps this is why I felt a faint glow of adolescent pride at our undesirable status. The barman had one of those old, fanatically grizzled druggie faces, and his dull eyes did not regard us at all sympathetically. I couldn't take issue with him because my gullet was clogged with gag-inducing mushrooms, which I was trying to swill down with the remaining drops of water from Dazed's bottle of Evian, but evidently the three of us collectively registered sufficient surprise to generate some kind of explanation from the barman.

'I don't want you puking,' he said.

'Several things,' said Amsterdam Dave, who had succeeded in swallowing his mushrooms. 'First, at my age, I do not need lessons in how to behave. I am a very civic-minded person. Second, my friends and I have a combined age of almost a hundred and fifteen years and we have, I think it's fair to say, no intention of throwing up. Third, if we do feel like throwing up, we'll make sure we step either outside or into the toilet. Fourth, if we are going to throw up it's not going to happen for at least half an hour. In the meantime, perhaps you would be so good as to bring us three coffees.'

It was an extremely impressive speech and, for a moment, I thought the barman was going to oblige. Then, with no alteration of expression, he clicked his fingers, pointed to the door and uttered two words. The first was 'Asshole!' The second was 'Out!'

'There is a world elsewhere,' I said to him with all the dignity I could muster – almost none – as we headed for the door. It didn't really matter, getting booted out like this. We simply took our custom elsewhere and went somewhere else. That's basically all we did for the rest of the day. We kept going elsewhere. It was rainy outside and each time we went outside we started thinking about getting inside again. At first this wasn't a problem because it wasn't raining. Oh, it was *raining* all right, but compared with the way it rained later this was nothing, this was clement. There was even a glimmer of sunshine. The leaves – the ones left in the trees, I mean; those lying on the ground in heaps were a different kettle of fish altogether – glowed in the brief intervals when the sun was shining, but even when the sun was not shining it was relatively pleasant.

Conditions deteriorated later on, but at this early stage of the day our main concern was the nauseous canker of doubt put into our minds by the surly barman. We kept expecting to feel sick, and then, when we no longer kept waiting to feel sick, we kept going somewhere else. First, though, we ordered three coffees in another, almost identical bar, where we waited to feel sick. When that didn't happen we went somewhere else. The sky was silvery grey, there was cloud activity, movement, variant shades of grey, the possibility of things improving. The day had not settled into the unanimous grey pall that indicated things were not going to get better until several days after we left, possibly not until next spring, by which time we would be long gone and anything that happened here would be long forgotten except by the one or two people – probably only one, possibly only me – whose business it is to make sure that such things are not forgotten, even if that means they have to be reinvented from scratch.

At some point conditions began to deteriorate. The wind picked up. It began raining heavily, and then, once it had begun raining heavily, some kind of maritime gale kicked in. We wanted to get out of the wind-whipped rain, but in order to get out of the rain it was necessary to continue walking in it, at least for a while. We headed for the relative tranquillity of the van Gogh Museum, where the paintings pitched and reeled in a blaze of yellow. Not that we saw anything of them. Conditions had deteriorated to the extent that everyone in Amsterdam had just one aim in mind: to get out of the rain, to get out of the rain and into the van Gogh Museum. Everyone was wet and steaming and at any moment a soggy stampede seemed a distinct possibility. Occasionally, in the background, a sunburst over the writhing corn of Arles, a Roman candle night – starry, starry – swirled into life. Blossom-tormented trees reared into view, pigment-coloured faces beamed brightly, but mainly there were just the drenched backs of museum-goers in their foul-weather gear, jostling for position. The thirsty yellow of Arles emphasized that here, in Amsterdam, it was the kind of autumn day that is all but indistinguishable from the dregs of winter. More and more visitors were crowding into the museum. The paintings were like the last lifeboats on the *Titanic*, and only a lucky few were going to get a glimpse of a gawking sunflower or Gauguin's empty chair (which, for all we knew, was not even there). Everyone else had to take their chances with the drawings or any other bit of art that floated their way.

The mushrooms, mercifully, were not as strong as they might have been, and before long we were out in the rain again. Incredibly, conditions had deteriorated still further while we had been in the museum; the weather, to cut a long meteorological story short, had gone from bad to worse to even worse.

'It's like being on the deck of a trawler in the North Sea,' I said. 'Were we not on dry land I would give the order to abandon ship.'

'Aye aye, sir,' said Dazed. We pressed on, heads bowed, heading for some other kind of shelter.

'Is it the season of mists and mellow fruitfulness?' Dazed asked as we battled through the rain.

'I suppose it is, technically, but I'm beginning to suspect that this is one of those places where they don't even have autumn. Each year they just plunge headlong from spring into the worst winter in living memory.'

'Is it the time of the falling fruit and the long journey to oblivion?' said Dazed.

'It really might be.'

'Do you think this might be a nice café?'

It did indeed look like a nice café, but once we were inside we became entangled in an impenetrable thicket of chairs. We couldn't move for chairs. With the van Gogh experience still reasonably fresh in our minds, it seemed as if Gauguin's empty chair had cloned itself and taken up permanent residence in this café. Amsterdam Dave's analysis of our situation was less art-historical, more pragmatic.

'Normally in cafés it's difficult to get a chair,' he said. 'Here there are too many chairs.' He could not have put it more succinctly if he had tried. There was an hilarious surfeit of empty chairs, so many, in fact, that there was no room to sit. We kept moving them, but as soon as we had moved one chair, another was in the way. Eventually we managed to create a space in which we had only three or four chairs each, not a bad ratio for those who are weary and damp of limb. We stretched out, ordered refreshments from a punky waitress who was either oblivious to or unperturbed by the superabundance of seating.

'Excuse me,' said Amsterdam Dave when she returned with our drinks. 'We were just wondering. Does it seem to you that there are rather a lot of chairs here?' Although Amsterdam Dave had addressed this question to the waitress, it was of course intended entirely for our benefit and amuse-ment. And find it amusing we did. Very much so. Weepingly so. Ha ha. We couldn't stop laughing. The more we tried to stop laughing, the more we had to laugh. As far as we were concerned it was just about the wittiest question in recorded history, a truly wonderful remark, right up there with anything ever said by anyone. Good old Amsterdam Dave. Having got us kicked out of one café, he was now in the process of getting us thrown out of a second. I struggled to get a grip on myself. I thought of the horrible conditions outside, I thought of us walking in the freezing horizontal rain, I avoided making eye contact with the others, concentrated on thanking the waitress and murmuring nonspecific apologies on our behalf. Then, when the waitress had gone off (in something of a huff), we subsided into giggles, wiped the tears from our eyes, and succeeded in getting a grip on ourselves.

In the wake of our giggling spasm I recalled that in the morning I had made an impulse purchase of a pair of trousers. Remembering this, I assumed that I had lost them in the course of our journey through the storm-ravaged streets of Amsterdam but, miraculously, they were here beside me, in a bag. I decided, there and then, to change out of my wet trousers, which were soaking cold and wet, and into my new ones, which were dry and lovely and warm. In the cramped confines of the toilet I had trouble getting out of my wet trousers, which clung to my legs like a drowning man. The new ones were quite complicated too in that they had more legs than a spider; either that or they didn't have enough legs to get mine into. The numbers failed to add up. Always there was one trouser leg too many or one of my legs was left over.

From the outside it may have looked like a simple toilet, but once you were locked in here the most basic rules of arithmetic no longer held true. Two into two simply would not go. It was insane, it took a terrible toll on my head. I concentrated hard, applied myself with a vengeance to the task in hand. I got one leg in. I got the other in. Hooray! A man who has finally put behind him the spectre of thirty years of unwanted celibacy – I'm in! – cannot have felt a greater surge of triumph and self-vindication than I did at that point.

Such exultation was short-lived, however, for these trousers were wet too. Somehow, I had put back on the wet pair that I had just taken off. The dry ones were still dry, waiting to be put on. I was back where I started. After all the effort of the last – how long? I could have been in here for hours – this was a crushing blow, and one I was not sure I could recover from. How had it happened? Human error, that was the only possible explanation. Human error. Somehow, evidently, I had taken off my wet trousers and put them on again. There was no other explanation, but what a huge mystery, what a maze of possibilities is contained by that innocuous 'somehow'.

Undeterred – or more accurately, almost entirely deterred – I started again. I extracted my long limbs from the wet pair and carefully eased them into the dry pair. This time, after much effort, I succeeded in putting them on back to front. By now I was so resigned to failure, to disappointment and frustration, that I scarcely even stopped to consider what had gone wrong (human error again, almost certainly). Without pausing I tugged them off and, head reeling from the effort, put them on again – only to find that I had put them on inside out. In other, less trying circumstances this might have seemed a fairly poor show for a forty-two-year-old intellectual but, as things stood, I was happy to regard it as a qualified success, especially as someone was now banging on the door, claiming I'd been in there for ages, wanting to know what the problem was.

'Good question!' I called back, in high spirits again, stuffing my wet trousers into the bag. All things considered it would have been a high-risk venture – who knows what new permutation of disarray might have resulted? – to have attempted to get my new trousers off and on. They might have been inside out but they were on, they were on, that was the important thing.

Back in the café, surrounded by a sea of chairs, Dazed and Amsterdam Dave were unconcerned by the state of my trousers. Already, just seconds later, it seemed hard to believe that I could have run up such an enormous bill of difficulties back there in the changing room. It was another world, that toilet, practically a different universe, one with its own extra-ordinary set of problems and obstacles. A piece of sophisticated electronic music came and went on the sound system, subsiding in a long ambient wash that made a peaceful resolution of human difficulties seem a distinct, almost inevitable possibility. What with one thing and another we were all a bit bedraggled, but the café was quite a cosy place to marshal our resources or whatever.

Quite suddenly, Amsterdam Dave said, 'By the way, did you know your trousers are inside out?'

'No, they're not,' I said.

'Yes, they are,' said Dazed.

'Well that's where you're both wrong,' I said. The inter-
lude of sitting quietly in the café had enabled me to see my
earlier difficulties in the toilet in an entirely new light and
to hold my own in any debate, however fiercely contested.
'It might look to you – to outsiders, as it were – as if my
trousers are inside out, but they are fine. *I* have turned inside
out.'

'That's quite a controversial analysis,' said Amsterdam
Dave.

'Controversial but, from my point of view, entirely
correct. And now, if you don't mind, I would like to discuss
something else.'

'Like what?'

'Like what we do next.' I was all for moving on somewhere else, you see. The others were quite content here but
I was all for moving on somewhere else. Somewhere new and
possibly better. I was restless, and who knows the part played
in this restlessness by the fact that my trousers were – however
strenuously I may have denied it – inside out? Was that why
I was so anxious to shift us from inside the café to outside on
the streets before returning inside once more? All things
considered, this was an excellent place, but I kept wanting to
move on, kept wanting to go somewhere else.

'What I want,' I said, 'is a place where we can sit down,
where we can just chat for a couple of hours before we go to
Matt and Alexandra's lavish suite. A place with nice music,
comfortable seats, and nice tea and so forth.' I went on and
on about this and, as I did so, I had a dim sense that I was
working through something, some neurosis that refused to
manifest itself plainly. And then it came to me.

'D'you know,' I said, 'I have just described exactly the place we're in. I'm already *in* the place I want to go to.'

'Well done, darling,' said Dazed. 'You've escaped from samsara.'

And so I had. I had unblocked all sorts of café chakras and was experiencing a sense of absolute calm. I was happy to be here in this chair-intensive café in the autumn of my drug-taking years, with my soon-to-be-ex-girlfriend, Dazed, who a few weeks later would succumb to one of her periodic bouts of severe depression, and my old friend Amsterdam Dave, whom I had met only the night before and who, months later, would himself – like the author of the present memoir – go completely to pieces. For the moment, though, we were happy to be where we were, confident in the knowledge that we would soon be basking in the comfort of Matt and Alexandra's lavish suite at the 717.

We turned up there exactly on time, on the stroke of six, and were shown up to Matt and Alexandra's suite by a quite charming waiter.

'Would you be so kind as to follow me?' he said, politely ignoring the fact that we looked liked some things the cat had dragged in and one of those things had its trousers on inside out. Matt and Alexandra's suite was every bit as lavish as we had hoped. It was a different world in there. That is something I remember distinctly about our weekend in Amsterdam: there really was a world elsewhere. Everywhere we went was like a different world from where we had just come from. Matt and Alexandra's lavish suite was like the world of Henry James, where sentences last for several paragraphs and fine glasses of red wine reflect, dimly, the flicker of the fire, the skewed outlines of framed portraits of men in ruffs. It was horrible outside, on the streets, but from here, from inside, it was a lovely autumn evening.

The suite filled up with Matt and Alexandra's other friends, but there was plenty of room for everyone, it being a suite. Matt opened the presents everyone had given him. Ours was wrapped up nicely in gold paper with a pale lemon ribbon because Dazed has a knack for doing things nicely, of making things special. If it had been left to me I would have given it – a critically acclaimed novel by a woman half my age – to him in the Waterstones bag it came in at Gatwick. In the bathroom I took off my trousers and put them back on correctly, inside in, with no difficulties whatsoever. We stretched out on sofas, drank glasses of fine wine, looked out of the windows at the gale-lashed trees. I hoped that conditions would deteriorate still further, that the rain would turn to sleet, because that would make being inside even nicer, even cosier.

I had known Matt for almost twenty years, and I felt so happy being with him in all this lavish cosiness that I could quite easily have wept. I think I did weep, actually. I felt happy, content; there was nothing I wanted. It didn't matter at all what one did with one's life, I decided. As long as you had evenings like this, the fact that one (I kept switching between 'one', 'you', and 'I') had accomplished next to nothing – none of that made any difference. It was better being forty than twenty, when one was full of fire and ambition and hope. It was even better than being thirty, when those hopes that had once animated you became a goading source of torment.

'Once you turn forty,' I said to Matt, 'the whole world is water off a duck's back. Once you turn forty you realize that life is *there* to be wasted.' I was so taken by what I had said – by its maturity, insight and wisdom – that I rambled on like this for quite a while, either to Matt or to myself, as I lay on one of several sofas, gazing at my old and new friends and other people in the group I had only smiled at and said hello to. Oh, it was a lovely evening, and then, quite suddenly, it was over, or this phase of it was anyway. Somehow we were all out on the streets again, walking through the UV haze of the hookers' windows in the red-light district that might better be termed the black-light district. A guy in an Arctic parka said something to me I did not quite catch, then I realized he was offering me drugs, specifically Viagra. I said I didn't want any.

'You look like you need it,' he said. It was an unkind remark but I pushed it to one side of my mind. Some of our party, including Matt and Alexandra, had already said good-night and headed off to bed. Those of us who were left went into a bar and smoked some feverish skunk, and then there were just the three of us again, Dazed, Amsterdam Dave and I, and we were no longer in the bar but out on the streets, back, in a sense, where we started. Under the influence of this hydro-whatever-it-was grass, the mushrooms, which had not worked very powerfully during the afternoon, made an unexpected comeback, and all the accumulated confusion of the day burst in upon us and left us stranded in an alien city that bore only an occasional resemblance to the Amsterdam of maps and guidebooks.

We were completely deranged, unsure of our bearings, utterly unsuited to the task of finding our hotel. One moment we were walking up a narrow, canal-bordered street, heading towards a church, say, and the next the church was nowhere to be seen and we were looking in the window of an antique shop. And then – improbably – we were in an antique shop, looking out at the three bedraggled figures peering in at renovated chairs, old maps, and dark desks on which yellow lamps encouraged a life of contemplation and study. The situation was complicated by the way that many of the homes we saw – uncurtained, softly lit, full of furniture, unpeopled, there for all to see – looked like antique shops, and vice versa. The distinction between residence and retail outlet was nothing like as clear as one might have imagined.

Other distinctions proved equally hard to sustain. We crossed a bridge only to find that we had crossed back over the bridge, which turned out to be a completely different bridge from the one we had been on seconds earlier. At various points I completely lost track of where in the world we had fetched up. It seemed to me that I was in six or seven cities at once. I was in Sydney, in the area known as King's Cross, which meant I was also in the area of London of that name and, at the same time, I was unable to get my bearings because what I saw persuaded me that I was in Paris and Copenhagen. I was everywhere at once.

'There is some place I have not yet been to,' I said in a blur of absolute lucidity, 'some place of which every other place has been no more than a premonition. But how will I know I'm there? If I can't answer that question, then for all I know I could be there already.'

How easy it was to become confused in Amsterdam, on that autumn night in Amsterdam particularly.

'What we must do,' said Amsterdam Dave, 'is concentrate on finding our hotel.'

'Of course we should,' I said. 'Of course we should. But the phrase "Easier said than done" comes to mind.'

'Here's a canal,' said Dazed, as though that solved everything, as though we had not seen hundreds of canals – or this very same canal hundreds of times – in the course of what was starting to seem a long and ill-advised excursion. Nevertheless, we gazed at this canal with baffled wonder and, for a moment, it seemed as if all our problems were over. But then we saw that it was indeed the same canal – dank with fallen leaves but glowing in spite of everything – that we had walked past either ten minutes or several lifetimes ago. Even more demoralizing – I am tempted to say soul-destroying – was the fact that if it had been a different canal, this would not have improved our situation in the slightest.

'Same canal, different canal,' I said forlornly. 'Same difference.'

'Well, I gave it my best shot,' said Amsterdam Dave as we looked up at the inscrutable calligraphy of a Japanese restaurant. 'Personally I'd be more than willing to cut my losses and settle for a plate of sushi.'

'You need a sharp knife for sushi,' said Dazed.

'That's not all you need,' I said.

'What else do you need?'

'Ah, you've got me there.'

'Fish,' said Dazed. 'You need fish.'

'Yes, of course. Fish,' said Amsterdam Dave. 'Fish – and a very sharp knife.' All the time we were talking nonsense like this we were also on the trudge, of course, walking, walking.

'For a moment back there I thought I was in Copenhagen,' I said. 'But now I realize that I feel like a Danish businessman, someone in telecommunications, who finds himself more than a little drunk in . . . in . . . Oh, I almost had it then. I almost knew exactly where we were. To the centimetre practically. How maddening it all is, this infernal not knowing. I feel I could just sit down and lament my entire life, every single moment of it.'

Was it still raining? Yes, in the sense that the air was full of moisture; no, in the sense that this moisture could not be said to be falling with any real conviction. It would be more accurate to speak in terms of a very light drizzle, so light that it was a species of mist.

'It makes places look welcoming but it does not make them any easier to find,' said Amsterdam Dave, who, I realized, had hacked into my private thoughts. Without really deciding to, we had sat down on a bench, not sat down on it as such (it was damp) but gathered in its vicinity.

'Would you say conditions had deteriorated?' Dazed asked sweetly.

'No,' said Amsterdam Dave. 'But I would say that our ability to cope with conditions has undergone a near-catastrophic deterioration.'

'Is there any point in looking at the map?'

'Actually that needs to be rephrased. The question is, "Is there any point looking *for* the map?"'

'Don't tell me we've lost the map. Without that map we're totally sunk.'

'I didn't say we'd lost it but I think we may have trouble finding it.'

'Let's put it like this. If we had the map would there be any point in looking at it?'

Dazed said, 'It might help us clarify a few things,' but Amsterdam Dave was adamant.

'Definitely not,' he said. 'We're much better off relying on instinct.' With that we were up and off, on the trudge again.

'Is it still the season of mists and mellow fruitfulness?' said Dazed.

'Yes it is,' I said. 'And equally, no it's not.'

'Is it still the time of falling fruit and the long journey to oblivion?' asked Dazed.

'I can't say,' I said. 'I really can't say.'

'Do you crave oblivion, darling?'

I confessed that at this moment I did, yes; that at this juncture I hoped the journey might not be so long after all. As soon as I said this, however, I became confused as to where we were heading.

'Is our hotel really called Oblivion?' I said. 'That's a strange and slightly ominous name, don't you think, the Hotel Oblivion? Is it really the kind of place we should be staying at? I mean, if that's what it's really called, fine. But I think we need to be sure.'

'You know,' said Amsterdam Dave, 'I don't think we're ever going to find it, whatever it's called.'

'Oh don't be such a pessimist,' said Dazed.

'I'm not sure it even exists any more,' said Amsterdam Dave.

'Oblivion?' I said. 'Are you saying that there is no such thing as oblivion?' It was a terrible prospect – it meant we were doomed to the glare of perpetual consciousness with no possibility of relief – but it was also a ridiculous one.

'If we assume that the hotel doesn't exist,' Amsterdam Dave continued, 'then that puts our situation in a totally different perspective. If that's the case, then we can just check in somewhere else.' I heard what he was saying but I was not really listening. The consequences of our hotel not existing were beginning to make themselves felt, and I felt all sad. I started thinking about the things that I had left in our room. I couldn't remember what they were, but if the hotel no longer existed, then probably they didn't either, and I was far from ready to kiss them goodbye, whatever they were. And if the hotel had stopped existing before we had officially checked out, where did *that* leave us? Were we a species of the undead, doomed for a certain time to wander Amsterdam in search of lodgings we were unable to enter? In this light, since the consequences of the hotel not existing were identical to there being no such thing as oblivion, it was logical to conclude that we were indeed looking for the Hotel Oblivion. I looked at Amsterdam Dave and Dazed but, from their faces, was unable to discern whether I had said all this or simply thought it.

Then, without warning or – as far as I could tell – justification, Amsterdam Dave said, 'Contrary to my previous announcement, I now think we're going to be home in less than twenty seconds.'

'Why do you say that?'

'Because there, about ten yards ahead, is our hotel.' I looked up and there, in pale blue letters, was the name of our hotel, just visible through the mist.

It was a moment of heart-stopping happiness. I was so relieved. All our troubles were over. Imagine, then, our confusion when we got to the door and realized that we had made a mistake, that it was not our hotel but a different hotel with the same name. It was incredible but, in the context of our experiences, all too possible, inevitable even. It was also, for me personally, the last straw. I couldn't bear any more of this nonsense, couldn't bear any of this confusion any more. I didn't know what to do. I was at the end of my tether, emotionally and physically. At my age I shouldn't even have been getting fucked up like this; I should have been at home in one of the many interiors we had glimpsed in the course of our walk, toiling away at some lamp-lit desk. I was about to start blaming Dazed and Amsterdam Dave for everything that had happened or not happened in the course of this wretched and stupid weekend. Then Amsterdam Dave tried his key in the door and the door opened and we realized that it may have been a mistake to have concluded that we had made a mistake, that although it did not look like our hotel, perhaps it was our hotel after all, and even if it wasn't, it was a good sign, surely, that the key worked.

LEPTIS MAGNA

Towards the end of the twentieth century, while living in Rome, I became conscious of what used to be called the grandeur of antiquity. One day my friend Monica – who, in the course of an afternoon at Hadrian's Villa, had told me she was born in Tripoli – showed me half a dozen black-and-white photos of her mother and father, in their early twenties, courting in some Roman ruins on the Mediterranean coast of Libya. These images of an ideal colonial romance showed her father, Mario, in a white shirt and pleated grey trousers, and her mother, Anna, in a white dress. They were tanned and wearing sunglasses, leaning against columns, perched on chunks of antiquity. The grey sky looked amazingly blue. In one picture Mario had his arm around Anna's shoulders, in another they were holding hands. Often the sea could be seen in the background. In front of them – behind the photographer's back (visible in one picture as a long snake of shadow) – was, I imagined, the desert, the huge beach of the Sahara.

What was it called, I wanted to know, this buffer of ruination between sea and desert?

'Leptis Magna,' said Monica.

There may have been other, equally impressive, more accessible ruins in Syria, Turkey or Tunisia, but from that moment, Leptis became the glamour ruin, the epicentre of antiquity. Leptis Magna: the four syllables were as much summons as name. As soon as I heard them I knew I had to go there, to see it for myself.

The years passed and I did nothing of the kind. It was almost impossible to go to Libya until the Lockerbie bomb suspects were handed over, until the Libyan authorities apologized for shooting British policewoman Yvonne Fletcher from a window in their embassy in London. Tours were occasionally arranged for those with a special interest in archaeology or schlepping across the Sahara, but there was no chance of going to Libya as an independent, unshepherded visitor.

Then, suddenly, it *was* possible. After the intervention of Nelson Mandela, the Lockerbie suspects were handed over for trial in the Netherlands under Scottish law. The Libyans apologized about Yvonne Fletcher. Britain reciprocated by denying claims about an MI5 plot to whack Gaddafi. Relations became friendlier. British Airways began flying direct to Tripoli.

It may have been possible to go to Libya, but it was still highly unusual. Even when I had arranged a visa and booked a flight, information about travelling there was hard to come by. There were dozens of guides to neighbouring Egypt and Tunisia, none to Libya. I couldn't even buy a map or book a hotel. I had bought a book about Leptis but, despite my fascination with the place, couldn't bring myself to read more than the first couple of pages, couldn't follow the story of the founding of the city, its history, its architectural features, its glory and subsequent decline. It was built on the site of a Phoenician settlement, sometime between the prehistoric days of Raquel Welch's fur bikini and the chariot race in *Ben-Hur*. That much is certain. The amphitheatre was inaugurated in about A.D. 1 (an easy date to remember) and was granted colonial status under the emperor Trajan in A.D. 109. The really spectacular monuments were built in the reign of Septimius Severus (193–211). After that, apart from getting trashed (by the Vandals?) in 523 and reclaimed by the Byzantines a few days later (relatively speaking), it was a complete blank.

Sitting on the plane, I wondered if there were any limit to my unpreparedness. Since living in Rome I had read quite a bit about the emperors and their atrocious appetites, but beyond this, the defining feature of antiquity was how uninteresting it was to read about. ('In the end you are tired of that world of antiquity,' wrote Apollinaire in his poem 'Zone'. 'You have had enough of living in Greek and Roman antiquity.') I am no stranger to boredom. I have been bored for much of my life, by many things but, equally, I have also been fantastically interested by many other things. Antiquity represented a weird synthesis – a kind of short circuit – of these two currents of my life: for the first time ever I was bored by what I was interested in. I didn't fight it. I would go to Leptis not knowing anything about it. For classicists and archaeologists a visit to Leptis was probably the summit of a lifetime's study, but I was an archaeologist only in the linguistic sense: I dug the past. Perhaps it was better that way. Auden certainly thought so. In 'Archaeology' he declared,

Knowledge may have its purposes,
but guessing is always
more fun than knowing.

I was intending to go further still and put my faith in the power not of guessing but of *ignorance* as an investigative tool. Where Foucault proposed an archaeology of knowledge, my trip to Leptis would proceed in the opposite direction: the archaeology of ignorance.

There were precedents of a kind. Ruskin remembers spending an afternoon driving about Rome, seeing 'the Forum, and the Colosseum, and so on. I had no distinct idea of what the Forum was or ever had been, or how the three pillars, or the seven, were connected with it, or the Arch of Severus . . . There was, however, one extreme good in all this, that I saw things, with whatever faculty was in me, exactly for what they were . . . What the Forum or Capitol had been, I did not in the least care.'

I was encouraged by this but unsure if it was true. Do you see things if you don't know what they are? Obviously a vocabulary of architecture is essential if you are to articulate what you have seen in a building, but perhaps the act of seeing itself is dependent on that lexicon. Without words are you not only mute but partially blind too? Was I going to Leptis to *not* see it? Alternating between confidence and extreme doubt, I felt myself on the brink of methodological panic. Gradually, as this panic deepened, I felt my confidence returning.

It's odd that panic has such a bad name. Most of the body's responses are rooted in a biological need to ensure the survival of the species. Even pain has its part to play. Panic, presumably, was designed with a view to extricating oneself from danger – so why is it that in any potentially dangerous situation we are instructed not to panic? If this plane were to ditch in the Mediterranean we would be urged not to spend our final seconds panicking but to go to our deaths calmly, in the brace position, wishing we'd paid closer attention to the emergency evacuation demonstration. But I was already in a panic and the panic generated its own kind of intensely agitated calm. It didn't matter at all that I had learned nothing about Leptis before coming here. The best way to learn was by looking, to become articulate in the language of sight. The eye could learn to look after itself.

Besides, no one else on the flight to Libya was troubled by such things. They were all travelling there on business (telecommunications, oil, computers), and most were drinking a fair bit too (beer, wine, spirits), stocking up in anticipation of forthcoming abstinence, which began as soon as we entered Libyan airspace.

The flight attendant's touchdown announcement – 'Welcome to Tripoli international airport . . .' – had never sounded more obligatory. Although she went on to inform us of the local time, one suspected that it was followed by an inaudible subtext along the lines of 'Not that it matters to us! As soon as this baby's got a bellyful of fuel we are outta here!'

By their airports shall ye know them! Because airports are on the fringes of non-space, their design is broadly similar the world over. Of all forms of architecture, the international airport is probably the least susceptible to regional variation. For this reason the tiniest details are disproportionately revealing about the country in which they are situated. Seasoned travellers can probably tell everything about the country they are in simply by the design and state – availability, condition, price – of the luggage trolleys. And the global uniformity of airports amplifies the extreme differences in atmosphere.

Tripoli airport was smoky. Not simply because people were smoking (though they were, of course; Libyans smoke like Turks) but, just as some new Parisian cafés are designed to exude instant tradition, so Tripoli airport seemed to have been designed in such a way as to anticipate the effect of ten, twenty, thirty years of heavy smoking. The style was smoked: 1970s smoked, to be exact. The whole place had a dull chrome, smoked glass feel about it. So smoked, so dull, in fact, that the chrome might well have been wood. The glass looked woody, the chrome looked woody. Now that I think about it there may not have been any chrome anywhere. Certainly there was none of the shininess associated with chrome and, oddly, it was this absence that made me think that chrome was somewhere in evidence. There was a lack of shininess – a woody quality – about the place which suggested nothing else so much as chrome. It was as if by some process akin to that by which forests turn eventually to oil, what had once been chrome had become wood. What I am trying to say, I suppose, is that the airport looked like it had seen better days, but it was impossible to imagine a time – even on the day it opened, in fact – when this had not been the case.

Perhaps this is why the atmosphere was so sullen.

Obviously it is not the job of customs and immigration officials to serve as unofficial greeters, but it was hard to imagine the screws at a low-security prison offering less of a welcome. Any human activity, even the most routine, can be inflected with the attitude, the mentality, of the person performing it. Wherever you enter America, your passport is always stamped – however daunting the interrogation leading up to this moment of formal admittance – with a certain have-a-nice-day zest. The stamp, consequently, often appears on the page at a jaunty tilt. Here, the immigration official flicked through my passport as though turning the pages of one of those Anselm Kiefer books, the ones made of lead, each page weighing about half a ton and dense with unpalatable history. He didn't stamp it so much as *grind* the ink on to the page. This surprised me. Maybe it's not such a great career, but aside from turning people away, refusing them admittance and putting them on the next plane home, the highlight of the immigration official's job must surely be giving the page a good, hard stamp, a bureaucratic equivalent of a Prussian click of heels. This guy stamped it grudgingly, reluctantly. I repeat, he didn't stamp my passport, he ground it. I am not exaggerating. By chance, the ink bath had run out of ink and so my stamp was dim and patchy, as if I had only been partially admitted.

Offices in the West aspire to the ideal of paperlessness (what next? the *desk*less office?). In Libya – as in most parts of the developing world – the opposite holds true. The idea is to generate paperwork. The term could hardly be more apt. Paper is work. Paper is the big employer. Someone fills out a form (in triplicate), someone else files one copy, the other copy goes somewhere else to be filed by someone else, the third is retained by the customer for his records. The most insignificant transaction must be scrupulously recorded and logged, filed and stored, even, on occasion, retrieved. Pity the archaeologists of the future who unearth a stash of millions of receipts and chits for the most humdrum of errands. Years of painstaking research will reveal – what? That on the twentieth of January 2000 the occupant – name illegible – of room sixteen ordered a tonic water from room service? What impression will they form of the societies that produced this volume of paper? Imagine the scale of the catastrophe necessary to impart to these receipts and invoices the magic of a fragment of poetry on a sheet of parchment. I had filled out immigration forms and customs declarations; now I filled out forms – of a complexity and thoroughness usually associated with a mortgage application – for changing money. Having done this, I was at last ready to get a taxi – but, no, I had to fill out a form for that too.

Formalities completed, we zoomed along an immensely deserted freeway. There were billboards of Gaddafi looking, as always, slightly camp (a consequence, I suppose, of spending time in his famous tent), but these did not suggest the omnipresence of a dictator so much as the imminent appearance in concert of an ageing – no longer 'Cheb' – rai star. We sat, the driver and I, in that companionable silence which is the result of being able to speak no more than two or three words of each other's language. One of these words was 'hotel', which, I soon discovered, meant something like 'sensation of heart-sinking disappointment on arrival, often accompanied by bitter regret at ever having left home'.

I checked in. Ah, how deceptively simple that sounds. To do so I had to fill out a couple of hectares of paper. Part of the problem was that solitary travellers like myself were utterly unheard of in Libya. In most parts of the world, locals discovering a tourist in their midst will invariably tell you that their country – however wretched – is 'very beautiful'. In Libya the only reaction was one of astonishment that anyone could have chosen to come here. It simply didn't make sense. Not surprisingly, then, there were no maps in the hotel gift shop and, as far as I could make out, no gifts either.

Having exhausted the attractions of the lobby, I retired to my room to watch TV. I had been interested in Libyan TV ever since Gaddafi, as a sign of mourning for the death of an Arab leader, decreed that TV would be broadcast in black-and-white for several days. At first I thought this edict was still in place, but after fiddling with the aerial for a few minutes, I managed to coax a dim vestige of colour from the set. As far as I could make out there was only one channel, featuring a concert in the desert given by Bedouins, filmed at the pace of Antonioni. This segment lasted twenty uneventful minutes. Then the focus shifted to a different, equally dreary musical event. The one available channel was, apparently, a funda-mentalist version of MTV. Time, I decided, for dinner.

The restaurant was devoid of everything except a guy – the maître d' – who was sitting with his head in his hands. I was not surprised by this. Jobs in some parts of the world involve nothing more than a commitment to turning up and doing nothing for eight or nine hours. When your shift is over you go home and do nothing there as well. If your job is outdoors, then employment becomes indistinguishable from

173

loitering. If your job involves being indoors, then it is often indistinguishable from the most abject despair. On seeing that a prospective customer had entered the premises, he perked up in the sense that he completely ignored me. I asked if dinner was ready. Not until eight, he said.

I went back to my room and, in a mood of grim resignation, wrote about my experiences of Libya up to and including the moment when I looked up from my notes and was confronted, in the mirror above my desk, with the awful reality – grey hair, bulbous nose, scrawny neck – of my appearance. I have often been disappointed by my appearance, but I have never looked so utterly repulsive as I did then. It was as if all the hidden misery of my life had suddenly manifested itself. Either that or I happened to have glimpsed the version of myself – a version that I had not in fact hidden as thoroughly as I had imagined – that was routinely seen by everyone I encountered. A prophecy was in the process of being fulfilled. 'Life,' said the face in the mirror, 'is taking its toll. All the disappointment and regret, all the bitterness and rage that you have tried to keep hidden, is now breaking out, eroding the last patina of handsomeness and hope. You are no longer a handsome man. This is the fate of all those who place an undue value on physical attractiveness. You will become one of those people – one of the hundreds of people to whom you paid the bare minimum of attention simply because you did not like the way they looked.'

I looked down, went back to writing about how, although I had been in Libya only a few hours, I was already thoroughly depressed. You know that feeling when you first arrive in a new city? However tired you are, however shattered by the flight, you are impatient to get out and sample the streets, the life, the action. Here in Tripoli I was already looking forward to sampling the action on the plane home. I had no urge to leave the hotel even though the hotel was basically grim and the room grimly basic. Still, at least there was dinner to look forward to.

During my earlier, abortive attempt at dining, I had taken little notice of the restaurant; now, sat at a table beneath a *Titanic* chandelier – the size, roughly, of an inverted wigwam – I was able to take in the full scale of the place. It was huge. There were forty tables, but only three people were eating, none of them displaying even the slightest symptom of pleasure in doing so. The table-to-customer ratio was ten to one, the staff-to-customer ratio was three to one – and still the place was chronically understaffed. That is assuming, of course, that staff in a restaurant will in some way be involved in facilitating the preparation and delivery of food. Such an assumption was utterly unwarranted in this establishment. As far as I could make out, most of the staff here were employed simply to stand around looking bored, to set the morose example followed by the three chewers and slurpers who had arrived before me. Rarely have I seen people take their profession so literally as the aptly named waiters.

Eventually, however, I was able to coax some soup from one of their number. It was cold, cold as the sea. There are few things in the world more dispiriting than cold soup. If food is disgusting, its very disgustingness elicits a reaction of fierce outrage. But cold soup – it saps the spirit, saps even the capacity for indignation and complaint, and so, having mumbled '*Shoukraan*,' I simply sat and sipped my cold soup until I could bear it no longer and lay down my spoon to indicate that I was, as they say in America, done. The waiter did not seem at all surprised that I had left most of my soup, and took it away without comment.

Watching him trudge away, I suddenly saw the huge dining room in a new light. Across the Mediterranean, in Italy, cooking had been raised to the level of art; eating was at the heart of social, family, and romantic life. Here – and the achievement, in its way, was no less impressive – food and everything connected with it could not have been rendered more joyless. One must not exaggerate. Obviously the food in the gulag would have been of a far inferior standard but, in the circumstances, the daily ration of bread and porridge was probably the source of considerable pleasure. Here no pleasure was to be derived from any aspect of the meal, not from the food, the setting or the service, or – God help us – the atmosphere. A restaurant on the moon could not have had less atmosphere. The only part of the meal people pursued with any gusto was the sucking of teeth. In the clanging acoustics of the room this sound – a kind of *veech* – echoed around grandly.

I had eaten – more accurately not eaten – foul food before, in Romania, for example, but in Romania there was at least the option – obligation practically – of getting blind drunk. Here I was in a state of ultra-high alertness and there was no prospect of oblivion. Full of nutrition-free bread, I signed for the non-meal and returned to my room. Now that dinner, the highlight of the day, was over, my room seemed grimmer than ever. The air-conditioning was making a fearsome racket even though I had turned it off earlier in the evening. After fiddling with the thermostat for ten minutes I came to the conclusion that it was impossible to turn off the air-conditioning. I called reception and eventually someone came up to fix the thermostat. His approach was nothing if not direct. Having examined the thermostat for a few moments, he simply tore it out of the wall. It was easy to see why the country relied so heavily on foreigners to carry out work in telecommunications. The thermostat, however, was nothing if not resilient: although it was hanging from the wall by only a few wires, the air-conditioning continued to thump and clatter. The man used the phone, calling, evidently, for back-up. Within ten minutes a colleague arrived, equipped with a stepladder. The first man duly mounted the steps and began taking panels out of the ceiling. My mood had improved somewhat because I was at least subjecting my hosts to considerable inconvenience. Then a panel crashed to the floor in a cloud of what I took to be asbestos dust. I didn't care. The man on the steps fiddled with the exposed plumbing, and suddenly there was silence. The ceiling panels were replaced and, having lived up to their name, the maintenance men made their exit.

I lay in bed, preoccupied by the age-old questions of travel: why does one do it? what am I doing here? These questions generated a third: what do I want out of life? The answer to which was: to be back home, to stay put, to stay in, to put my feet up, to watch telly. For at least six months before coming to Libya I had been feeling what I suspected might be the tug of middle age. It manifested itself as a diminution of everything by which I had previously set the greatest store (vitality, appetite for new things, new challenges) and an intensifying wish for the familiar. There were times, watching football on TV, when I took solace in the fact that in one form or another football would be played, would be there to be watched, for the rest of my life. All I would have to do would be to sign up for some kind of cable or satellite package. The players would change, new stars would emerge, old ones would fade into the lower divisions or drop abruptly out of sight, but the games would remain pretty much the same. The results from this point of view were irrelevant; all that mattered was that the games would be played and I would be there on my sofa, beer in hand, watching. As I lay on my bed in Libya, with no beer within a hundred miles, this seemed as near to a vision of the afterlife – the injury-time life – as I was ever likely to come. In the meantime, though, there was the pre-afterlife – this life, or the first night of it anyway – to get through first.

I was so eager to see Leptis Magna that, in the morning, I took a taxi in the opposite direction. I wanted my experiences in Libya to climax with Leptis, so I thought it best to start out with a trip to Sabratha, the other antique attraction. My driver was of the Eastern, honking school. He liked to let people know he was there. He used his horn to greet, indicate, berate, acknowledge, urge, and warn. Had it been physically possible he would probably have steered with it too. I was struck by the subtle range of expression he was able to get out of it, from sustained single-note blasts to delicately inflected modulations of intent. With his horn he expressed his relation to the world and his views on that world. It was how he communicated. In this way we nudged and honked our way out of Tripoli and left the city behind.

At Sabratha the blue of the sea met the gold of the desert. The blue of the sky was not like the blue of the Bahamas, which is watery blue, nor was it like the blue of Arizona, say, somewhere miles inland, which is totally parched. The blue of the sky here was watery and parched and therefore utterly resplendent. It was also a wintery blue and the day was not yet warm.

A man in a suit and spectacles offered me a tour. The frames of his spectacles were thick and black, imparting to his face a look of the utmost gravitas. Ah, the lovely wisdom of heavily framed spectacles! Such spectacles, I imagined, were helpful in coaxing more tolerant and liberal readings from the Koran. No sooner had I thought this than I imagined the same glasses perched on the stern face of a cleric for whom any but the harshest, most unyielding readings were blasphemous. Through such glasses one could watch unmoved as a woman was stoned to death for chewing gum or see the exquisite sensuality of the sacred texts. It was impossible to draw any definitive conclusions, but the man wearing this particular pair of heavy black spectacles had a benign look about him, possibly because the spectacles – as was to be expected – were held together on one side by a piece of Sellotape.

I like countries where people continue to use things even when they are broken. Why throw them away? Why not keep wearing them till the lenses themselves wear out? These lenses looked like such a day would be millennia in coming. The eyes of several generations would stare themselves into the grave before these lenses registered the slightest wear and tear. To say they were milk bottle bottoms is to impart to them a slimness and delicacy they stoutly disdained. They were as thick as those moulded windows you sometimes see in English pubs. Behind them his eyes loomed and receded drunkenly. I like to look people in the eye but in this instance it was like looking into the eye of a hurricane.

I declined the offer of a tour. I was seized by a fierce impatience to see the ruins, as if these ruins, which had stood for however long, had to be seen in the next half an hour. Also I simply do not like tours. I detest being lectured at and told things, even by an amusing guide. I like going at my own pace, and besides, at some level I already knew everything – that is, nothing – about Sabratha that I would ever need to know, and if there was anything I didn't know that I felt I did need to know, I could look it up later, when I was back in the comfort of my own home, surrounded by books I did not yet possess.

From a distance the ruins of Sabratha did not seem so spectacular. Then the remains of the theatre reared up before me, glowing gold as toast. It looked baroque, like a duomo turned inside out, like something hung out to dry centuries before and long since forgotten. Three tiers of colonnades were heaped on top of one another. It was entirely vertical and there were so many gaps – windows, let's say – that the sky seemed weight-bearing, an essential part of the construction. Either that or the purpose of ruins was to frame the sky which was always there, a bright rectangle of nothing but blue. Every archway was a picture, massively framed, of the distance beyond. In turn this picture contained another arch, another view. Glimpsed through arches and windows, the sky was framed constantly by the theatre, which was in turn framed by the sky. In this way the structure was all the time offering new angles from which it and the sky could be viewed: new perspectives on the past.

Also – and this cannot be over-emphasized – it was a theatre where time, in the idiom of the stage, was enjoying one of its longest-ever runs. The auditorium had become the show and the show never changed, only the lighting – and that, of course, was part of the show. It was a classic perform-ance. I trod the boards of antiquity. The sky blazed. Everything was faded and sharp and glowing. The sky had nothing to do but be there, lording it over what it looked down on all day, day after day, including the nights. Speaking of the night, the moon showed up early. By three o'clock in the afternoon it was a definite presence. I've never had the slightest interest in the physics of the stars, or the myths suggested by the constellations, only in looking at them and not having any thoughts at all, just looking at the firmament, viewing the star footage or – in this instance – the daylit moon, which was simply this thing called the moon.

I walked round to the back, the seaward side of the theatre. From here it looked solid, like the impregnable wall of a Foreign Legion castle, a Beau Geste fort (a US cavalry fort, in other words, airlifted to the Sahara and surrounded by the ghosts of Apache Arabs). You would never have guessed – from this point of view – that it was just a shell, a movie set, effectively, left over from the antique heyday of costume drama. It looked real. I drifted away from the theatre into an area scattered with bits and pieces of antiquity. All that remained of the statue of Flavius Tullus was the folded drapery of a toga. Nothing was left of the body – no head, no arms – except the dependable feet, a subtle rejoinder to Rilke's 'Archaic Torso of Apollo': you must change your clothes!

Pale, mottled, the moon was floating in the windows and arches of the theatre. I went back there, back inside (insofar as a place with no ceiling has an inside). It was warm now. Near the stage were two carved dolphins looking like fish out of water. The stone glowed with the energy of all the centuries of sun that had shone down on it. A family walked on to the stage and then wandered off. The wood did its best to glow too. Certainly there was not such an abrupt distinction between wood and stone. Both had taken on some of the character of the desert to which they were determined – destined even – to return.

I had grown fond of my driver, but for one reason or another he was busy the next day, and the hotel organized a taxi to take me to Khoms, eighty miles east of Tripoli, the nearest town to Leptis. I suspected they had cheated me over the fare but went along with it anyway. I was too cast down by the rain to care about getting ripped off. Yes, it was pouring. It shouldn't have been but it was. There is a meteorological curse on me. Weather systems rearrange themselves around my presence. Fronts move in. Areas of low pressure build up. I arrive somewhere, it begins raining. Until yesterday, I am always informed, the weather had been perfect. Until yesterday there had not been a drop of rain for six weeks, not a cloud in the sky since records began. But if I am there it rains. The dry season becomes the wet season. When I was in Goa it rained on New Year's Eve. It rained in the desert at Burning Man. It rained in Lombok in June. And now, in Libya, having left Tripoli behind, we sped along the highway while the rain – tidal, almost – crashed around us. It was more like being on a trawler in the North Sea than a road on the edge of the desert.

There was no other traffic. I was like a president in a one-car motorcade. This is one of the OPEC ironies of the world. Many of the oil-producing nations have roads – and oil – but no traffic. They have exported not only their oil but their traffic problems too. I'd spent the evening before coming to Libya watching telly, four hours of it back to back, and the commercials had all been for cars. Nose-to-tail car ads. Singly, each had been selling you a car (gliding through the desert, dodging jams, leafing through country lanes), but such was the volume of car ads that even a child could see what was really on sale: traffic.

Here and there the torrential rain had flooded the road and we had to cross the meridian and drive along the west-bound lane, into the path of the oncoming traffic (of which there was none). Although he did this safely, I did not like my driver. He was young, smartly dressed in an overcoat and smart shoes. His hair was cut short, his lips had the dryness of the habitual smoker, and – though he tried hard to conceal it – he had the look of someone who was on to a good thing.

The nearest hotel to Leptis was the Al Jamih, a so-called tourist hotel. Already depressed by the rain, my spirits plummeted when I arrived there. It was a profoundly depressing place, infinitely more dismal than the dismal hotel in Tripoli. An atmosphere of the most appalling gloom hung over the lobby, where a few men were watching TV (it was eleven in the morning). Some of these were staff, none of them was doing anything or looked like they would be doing anything this side of eternity. I, on the other hand, embarked on the Tolstoyan task of checking in.

'Are you alone?' the desk clerk asked.

'Yes,' I said. 'Quite alone and deeply concerned about the weather.'

A couple of hours later the sun peeped out. It was still raining but the sun was shining. Then the rain stopped and the sun went in. For fifteen minutes it was a fifty-fifty, could-go-either-way stand-off. Then the sun came out again. This time it looked like staying out. Which it didn't. Then it did. The clouds skulked off, the rain moved inland, and I made my way to Leptis.

The entrance to the ruins was indicated by the arch of Septimius Severus: scaffold-clad, in the process of some kind of renovation – and therefore disappointing. Reminding us that the past's survival is not due entirely to its own stored reserves of longevity, scaffolding is fatal to the spell of antiquity. It gets – mediates – between the clean lines of ancient stone and the framing timelessness of the sky. I moved on, to the palaestra, an expanse of grass and scattered columns. Immediately there was the sense – which I've had in only a few places in the world – of entering not so much a physical space as a force field, a place where time has stood its ground. I first experienced it on the Somme, at Thiepval, and perhaps I've never felt it quite as powerfully anywhere else. Other people get a similar feeling when they step into a great cathedral, into Chartres or Canterbury, or just a church even. I assumed I'd never been able to feel it in such places because of a lack of – even a profound aversion to – the faith that inspired them. But equivalent places – mosques, synagogues – leave me cold also. (I feel more comfortable in Buddhist or Hindu temples, where the faith is so all-embracing that you could, if you feel like it, leave a cuddly Donald Duck at the altar without encroaching on the holiness – let alone the aesthetic harmony – of the place.) Then, in the Rothko Chapel in Houston, Texas, I had a revelation. In that famously non-denominational environment – a place designed to provide a setting for the contemplation of the spirit by those who, like myself, did not feel at home in any of the more traditional places of worship – I felt . . . nothing. Not a thing. If anything, it all felt slightly bogus. Pious even. I had plenty of time, was in no hurry. I sat there for a good while, surrounded by those impenetrable menus of the artist's soul, waiting for something to happen, willing on the blood-and-pigment epiphany. But there's no faking these things: either you have the great experience or you don't. I knew it was not going to happen. And then it did happen, in the sense that I realized it could never happen *indoors*.

D. H. Lawrence experienced a sense of arrival, of 'some-thing final', at Taos Pueblo. Some places felt temporary on the face of the earth, but Taos, Lawrence thought, retained 'its old nodality'. It was the same here, at Leptis. It was not a place I had entered, but the dream space of the past. I was in the Zone.

I always know when I'm in the Zone. When I'm in the Zone I don't wish I was anywhere else. Whereas when I'm not in the Zone I'm always wishing I was somewhere else, wishing I was in the Zone.

A narrow-gauge railroad track wound its way through the site (part, now, of the ruin whose excavation it had been designed to facilitate). The Hadrianic Baths were flooded by the recent rain. The surface of the waters was stirred by the wind. A few tins rusted at the bottom of the baths. Weeds writhed over broken tiles.

It was not surprising that these details came straight out of *Stalker*: I got the idea of the Zone from Tarkovsky but the Zone in *Stalker* is not the only Zone. If it weren't for *Stalker* I'm not sure I would ever have realized that the place I wanted to be – and the state I wanted to be in – was the Zone. Before I saw *Stalker* I only had the need, the longing. In some sense I might have been in the Zone prior to seeing *Stalker*, but part of being in the Zone is realizing you're in the Zone, and since I didn't know there was such a thing as the Zone, I was not really in it. That is the thing about the Zone, that is one of the things I love about it: I know when I'm there, and I knew I was in it in the Severan Forum.

Enclosed by four high walls and a vast lid of sky, the forum was completely hidden from view until I was inside it. In the palaestra I'd entered the force field of the past; here I was completely enclosed – sealed – within it, walled in. The feeling was all the more marked because of the scale of the place, so huge it was difficult to think of comparisons (so many basketball or tennis courts). Also, unlike the palaestra – open, sparsely columned – it was dense with debris. It looked, actually, like a storage room or warehouse for bits and pieces of antiquity awaiting sorting and export. As well as a jumble of pillars and plinths, limestone fragments had been stacked up in neat piles as though the site were about to be redeveloped as a Cotswold village (Leptis on the Wold) with authentic drystone walling. Alongside the perimeter wall were columns and colonnades. In places, the earlier rain had all but disappeared. Marble slabs which, an hour ago, had been drenched were now dry enough to sit on. Elsewhere the water lay several inches deep. The sun bounced off puddles, throwing shadow ripples on the surrounding stones, making them seem liquid, melty. One of the columns bathed in writhing shadow was filled entirely with writing. As soon as I had noticed this I became conscious of a man making his way slowly towards me.

'*Salaam alaykum!*'

'*Alaykum salaam!*' Shortly after this exchange we hit upon French as the best language in which to communicate.

'*Qu'est-ce que vous faites ici?*'

'*Je suis un touriste.*' Not for the first time this answer was greeted not with puzzlement but blank incomprehension.

'*Touriste?*'

'*Oui.*'

'*Avec un groupe?*'

'*Non.*'

'*Et vous êtes tout seul?*'

'*Oui,*' I said. '*Je suis tout seul.*' Perhaps it was because we were speaking French, but this question – *Vous êtes tout seul?* – had taken on what I am cheaply tempted to call an existential quality. Shortly before coming here I had split up with my girlfriend. I was all alone, had been alone much of my life, and would, in all probability, die alone. And it was, of course, speaking to another human being that brought this home to me. While I had been strolling on my own, I was quite happy, I was in the Zone. No sooner had I begun chatting with this fellow than I was burdened with the most terrible loneliness. That is another thing about the Zone; one moment you can be in it and the next moment you are no longer in it. You are just in some place, wishing something were different. I said goodbye to my new friend and walked on. I had to be on my own, just so that I would not feel so alone.

A bank of clouds moved swiftly across the ruins of the forum. The sky darkened, brightened, grew dark again. Perhaps it was not the clouds that were moving but the earth itself, going through the motions of its orbit at a furious pace. It was like experiencing time from the perspective of the ruins: years, decades, even centuries whizzing by like a day viewed through a time-lapse camera. For a short while the stones retained some of the glow that they had absorbed from the sun. Then, as the sky became uniformly grey, the stones faded, dulled. I felt disappointed, cheated. As the gloom settled I saw that I had spent the last fifteen years dragging the same burden of frustrated expectation from one corner of the world to the next. I felt I could no longer take the roller-coaster emotions of travel, its surges of exaltation, its troughs of despondency, its huge stretches of boredom and inconvenience. It was no longer pleasant sitting here in the forum, but the prospect of going back to the hotel was even more wretched. I wished there were someone I could talk to, but as soon as this wish was realized – I became aware that someone was standing next to me – I wished only to be left alone.

My new friend was called Ahmed and, after pausing for thought, he said, 'Manchester United . . . Leeds . . . Arsenal . . . Chelsea . . .'

'Tottenham Hotspur?' I prompted.

'Tottenham Hotspur,' he repeated. 'Newcastle United . . . Aston Villa.' After this brief revival he faltered again before embarking on a sub-set of the same conversational genre.

'Dennis Bergkamp,' he said. 'Kanu. Viera. Gascoigne . . . Zola.' This was proof, of a sort, that a new era had dawned, both in English football and – by extension – the international language of diplomatic relations. Until surprisingly recently the litany of names would have started with Bobby Charlton and petered out with Denis Law and George Best. There was little pause to consider the implications of this, however, for Ahmed was off again.

'Head,' he said pointing to his head. Then, pointing to his nose, 'Nose.' Then, 'Arm,' pointing to his arm. Next he said, 'Teeth.'

'Bad teeth,' I said cruelly. 'Yellow teeth.' The adjectives meant nothing to him. Ahmed existed in a world comprised exclusively of nouns.

'Trees,' he said, continuing to point. 'Stones.' He had no adjectives and no verbs, only nouns. It coincided with the way we had met: he had not walked towards me, had not approached, sauntered, or made his way over; I was simply and suddenly confronted by the fact of his presence. This rudimentary stage of linguistic development also anticipates the one where civilizations inevitably end up: all around were the vestiges of nouns – columns, stones, trees. No verbs remained. Doing – history – was over with. Consistent with his verbless view of the world, Ahmed showed no sign of moving, leaving or going. I became slightly suspicious of his motives, not because of any indication of ill intent, simply because there had to be some ulterior motive for persisting with a conversation of such appalling tedium. Although I had contributed to the dialogue – pointing to things, naming them – I was all the time in the grips of a boredom so intense that it threatened to turn into hysteria. Ahmed, by contrast, was entirely at ease, confirming something I had dimly suspected: in many parts of the world boredom simply does not exist.

Perhaps boredom is the distinctive quality of the modern Western mind. Always, in the West, there is a friction between the self and time; in Africa, India and Asia many people have a subsistence relation to time, taking it as it comes. On a train in Kerala I'd met a man a few miles into what was going to be a seventy-hour rail journey. He was completely unperturbed by the prospect. My own journey was going to last only three hours, I was thoroughly enjoying it – but I was already looking forward to it being over with. The more travel speeds up, the more acute this feeling becomes. When it took weeks or months to travel by ship from Europe to America, no one suffered these agonies of impatience. Increased speed has served mainly to accelerate our impatience at any delay. What will we wait for when it takes no time to get anywhere? Perhaps then we'll revert to the timeless, verbless inanition of Ahmed. Alternatively, only when everyone in the world is susceptible to boredom will the project of globalization be complete. In the meantime I'd had enough: I wanted to get back to the hotel I had no desire to be in.

* * *

Surprise, surprise! The hotel restaurant was closed. Not that it mattered. According to the receptionist there was a selection of restaurants in town. This selection amounted to a choice between four places selling roast chicken. I went into one, washed my hands at the sink opposite my table and avoided drying my hands on the filthy towel. I ordered half a chicken and ate some of it. It was not bad, I suppose, if you like that sort of thing – though why anyone would is beyond me. After dinner – to put it somewhat grandly – I walked back along the main drag. Mud and litter had formed a kind of garbage stew in the gutters. Cars clanked and lumbered by. People dragged themselves along, noticing the gangly stranger in their midst and taking no notice.

Back at the hotel I read for as long as I could and then got into bed. This involved a reversal of the normal preparation for sleep. Instead of taking off my clothes, I put more on to make sure that no part of me was in contact with the filthy sheets. This did not stop the smell – a combination of dirty feet and non-specific genital seepage – invading my nostrils, but I tried to reassure myself with the thought that you probably don't catch anything from smelling dirty sheets. All the time I was reassuring myself with this thought, however, I was seething with anger at the dirtiness, the casual acceptance of dirt, which, coupled with an unwillingness to provide anything remotely resembling service, was the defining feature of the hotel, even though it was, precisely, the opposite of these features – namely cleanliness and service – that made a hotel a hotel and not a filthy hovel offering the most rudimentary shelter against the elements. My thoughts were approximating a syntax of formal if delirious complaint; at the same time, however (in this context it was inevitable that the word 'however' make some kind of aggrieved appearance), they were undermined and animated by the knowledge that there was no one with whom such a complaint could be lodged, no higher authority to whom I could appeal. And so this simple grievance about sheets and dirt acquired an unanswerable, almost metaphysical quality and became, as I hovered on the grubby rim of sleep, a lament for the grimy, fallen condition of the world.

Apart from a few feathers of cloud, the sky, next morning, was perfectly clear. Birds were singing. The air was chilly, waiting to become warm as I made my way to Leptis again. Once there, I walked for hours without encountering a single person. It became hot. The moon appeared over the Arch of Trajan. At one point I found myself back in the Severan Forum and the adjacent basilica. Some columns sparkled a bit in the sunlight – the almost invisible remains of marble cladding long since stripped by erosion or thieves. That, I guessed, was the practical explanation. I preferred to think that the columns had been cast from such stuff, from such stuff as stars, from such stuff as stars are made of. And not only that. Just as stars are often stone-cold dead – no longer actually there – before their light reaches us, so what I was seeing now was the light of the extinct city.

I looked at my book on Leptis and again made little progress. One page featured an artist's impression showing what the city would have looked like in its glorious heyday. From this perspective what remains is a form of forensic evidence – a negative blueprint – of what was. The more meticulously they are done, however, the less convincing such reconstructions become: for me, antiquity is not what can be deduced but, exactly, what remains.

Leptis, in other words, only really got going when it fell into ruin; its decline was its glory (and vice versa). That is part of the consolation of ruins. It is impossible to visit the Riviera without wishing you had been there earlier, with Scott and Zelda in the twenties; or Anjuna when the first full-moon parties were held in the late eighties, when it wasn't raining. Ruins do not make you wish that you had seen them earlier, before they were ruins – unless, that is, they have become too ruined. Ruins – antique ruins at least – are what is left when history has moved on. They are no longer at the mercy of history, only of time.

The sea could not be heard. Everything had become still. This is what I had wanted: to experience history as geography, the temporal as the spatial. Wind is the breath of time, hurrying by. Stillness, though, is like the trance of stopped time.

Scattered columns, arches, statues. Ancient latrines. Olive trees. The whistling of birds. Columns against the flag of sea and sky, two flat bands of horizontal blue.

Virginia Woolf apparently told Rupert Brooke that the sky between leaves was the brightest thing in nature: a profoundly parochial remark in that it holds true only in the leafy context of Charleston or some English shire. The sky is brightest around the edge of antique columns. And no line is sharper than the one dividing a column from the sky that frames it. There is a simple, entirely irrational explanation for this: what separates the column from the sky has been worn down – has become thin and therefore sharp – over time. The sky is as close as can be while still remaining distinct. This absolute separation between the timeless man-made and the eternal is never as pure as it is in the ruins of Greek or Roman antiquity. That is one way of looking at it. The other – a different way of looking at the same thing – is that the distant past is brought into sharp adjacency with the present.

The ruins were bathed in a perpetual present of which the golden light and stalled moon were the perfect expression. I moved from place to place, arranging the intersections of columns, sea, and sky in new ways, new angles. Perhaps the simplest lesson of antiquity is that, after a time, anything vertical – Doric, Ionic, Corinthian, whatever – commands admiration. Ultimately, though, the lure of the horizontal will always prove irresistible. That's why the sight of the ancient vertical is always enhanced by a backdrop horizon of sky and sea. From their point of view – the point of view of sea and sky – Leptis was still in the early stages of a career of ruination which would end ultimately as desert, when the horizon would be undisturbed by any vestige of the vertical: the final triumph of space over time.

THE RAIN INSIDE

For reasons that aren't worth going into now, I once believed that the only way I was going to write a book I had almost given up all hope of writing was to go and live in Detroit. I'd had the idea for this book in Rome; it was going to be about the ruins of classical antiquity, but I'd gradually fallen into ruin myself. I couldn't read or write or do anything that required sustained attention. I was distracted, constantly, by one thing or another. Everything competed with and detracted from everything else. Nothing was satisfying, nothing held its own. If I was out I wanted to be in; if I was in I wanted to be out. At its most extreme I would think, I'll sit down, and then, as soon as I had sat down, I would think, I'll stand up, and then, as soon as I had stood up, I would want to sit down again. I spent my life sitting down and standing up. I felt like I was turning into Troy, the damaged guy whose fidgeting had afforded me so much amusement at the Sanctuary. I couldn't settle. Even if I did sit down successfully, even if I sat down and realized that sitting down was exactly what I wanted to do, still, within seconds, I would think of something else that would render sitting down even more satisfactory. I would decide that I wanted to supplement my sitting with a cup of tea, or by reading a particular passage of Yeats, or by listening to some music, and so, having sat down perhaps thirty seconds earlier, I would be up again, heading to the kitchen to make tea or to my study where something else would distract me and I would embark on another inessential, soon-to-be-abandoned task, so that by the time I actually returned to the sofa, the moment – the sitting-down moment – had passed and I no longer felt like sitting down, and I'd be up again, heading to the bathroom to check that I had turned the tap off properly. Or I'd go to the kitchen and open the window, then shut it and open the living room window instead – then shut that and reopen the one in the kitchen. Or pick up the phone to check that I had replaced the handset properly when I last picked it up to check that I had replaced it properly. I had become so habituated to this state of serial distraction that I scarcely gave it a second thought. Then I came across a passage in *Shadows on the Grass*, in which Isak Dinesen recounts a painter's description of a nervous breakdown he'd suffered during the First World War: 'When I was painting a picture . . . I felt that I ought to make up my bank account. When I was making up my bank account, I felt that I ought to go for a walk. And when, in a long walk, I had got five miles from home, I realized that I ought to be, at this very moment, in front of my easel. I was constantly in flight, an exile everywhere.'

Not for the first time I realized that I was continuing to function – continuing, more accurately, to malfunction – while in the grips of some kind of domestic shell shock or *pre*-traumatic stress, that I had been in the midst of an ongoing nervous breakdown without even being aware of it, that I had, in fact, gone to pieces. I mean that as literally as possible. Everything had become scattered, fragmented. I couldn't concentrate. Each day was scattered into a million pieces. A day was not made up of twenty-four hours but of 86,400 seconds, and these did not flow into one another – did not build, as letters do, into words and sentences – so that, as a consequence, there was not enough time to get anything done. My days were made up of impulses that could never become acts. Ten hours was not enough to get anything done because it wasn't really ten hours, it was just billions of bits of time, each one far too small to do anything with. That must be why I often went from room to room checking that all the clocks showed exactly the same time, sometimes going back to where I'd started because I had not taken into account the delay in getting from the kitchen to the bedroom by way of the living room and study. There was a stampede going on in my head, except what was going on in my head was worse than a stampede. A stampede occurs when a mass of animals moves in one direction; mine was a stampede in which everything flew off in every direction. Chaos theory, the big bang, entropy – all this physics, this primal chemistry or whatever it was, was all going off in my head all the time. The smallest setback threw me into a blind panic. I didn't have panic attacks – I was in a state of continuous panic. It wasn't that I couldn't concentrate – I was in the grips of something that was the opposite of concentration, a centrifugal force that created an irresistible sense of dispersal.

It was only when I conceived the idea of living in Detroit that my hopes of writing my book about classical antiquity were revived. In a sense my hunch was right in that I never did go to live in Detroit and I abandoned all hope of ever writing a book about classical antiquity – but in the midst of this period of serial distraction, I did go there, briefly, to cover the first ever Detroit Electronic Music Festival.

My trip got off to the worst possible start. I was packed and ready to go – but I couldn't find my sunglasses. I looked everywhere, I mentally retraced my steps, I telephoned places where there was the smallest chance I had left them even though I knew that I had not left them in any of these places. By the time I abandoned the search, my flat was a wreck and there was no denying the simple, terrible truth: I had lost my sunglasses. To say this was a blow is a considerable understatement. I loved those sunglasses. The prescription lenses were heavily polarized and tinted an oneiric red that made everything so much better – clearer, trippy, brighter – than it ever could have been without them. I'd had them made a decade earlier in New Orleans and practically everything I'd seen in bright sunshine since then I'd seen through them. I'm not interested in memories – I don't have a camera – but I need, absolutely, to be able to enter this dream space that makes everywhere in the world look slightly the same. Without them, Detroit – and not just Detroit, the *world* – would be a grey and dismal place.

I had avoided losing these sunglasses in countless situations in which they could quite easily have been lost. I'd been round the world several times in them and I'd never even been close to losing them. I'd worn them in Miami, Rome, Cambodia, Indonesia, Thailand, Paris, Black Rock City, Libya . . . I might not have had them on all the time but at some point in every one of these places I had worn those sunglasses.

It is only a slight exaggeration to say that I never let them out of my sight. It was those glasses that enabled me to formulate my basic rule for the preservation of spectacles: if they're not on your face, they should be in their case. I preached it and I lived it. I anticipated situations in which I might lose them and planned accordingly. I've never looked after anything like I looked after those sunglasses. And then, somewhere in England, I'd lost them. How did it happen? I've no idea. If I knew how it happened I'd know where they fucking were, wouldn't I? They were taken from me.

There is some kind of moral in this. Or not a moral but a fact. Things go missing. They just disappear. You invest your whole being in not losing something and still, incredibly, against all odds, you lose it. The more you covet something, the more certain it is that you'll lose it, and the more devastating this loss will be when it happens – which it will. So that's how it was now, that was the world – glaring, unfocused, harsh, blurred – through which I would pass like a ghost. No photograph could ever show the world as it appeared to me through those sunglasses. Their loss was absolute. I've tested other lenses since then but none has their peculiar depth and clarity. Wearing them was like taking a drug that immediately unveiled the psychedelic sublime. I would never see the world again as I saw it through those sunglasses.

They weren't just sunglasses, I realized as I drove from Detroit airport to my hotel; they were a way of looking at the world, a sensibility, almost a way of life.

The following morning, refreshed but still mourning the loss of my sunglasses, I drove to the Detroit Institute of Arts, a resplendent building packed with plunder from the Motor City's boom years. The main attraction was a large show of van Gogh self-portraits, some surprisingly Kirk Douglas-like and all of them, even the most despondent, colourful as the happiest days in the whole history of art. I had the feeling that I'd seen most of them before, at various museums round the world, particularly in Amsterdam (not just the time I was there with Dazed and Amsterdam Dave, when we'd got all messed up on mushrooms, but other times also). As well as the self-portraits there may have been some yellow pictures of flowers. In fact, now that I think about it, I am not entirely convinced that it was a show of self-portraits as such. Perhaps it was an exhibition of pictures by van Gogh from the Whatever Collection in Wherever, a substantial number of which were self-portraits. Not that it matters. It wasn't van Gogh that did it for me that afternoon, but Frederic Edwin Church. The painting was called *Syria by the Sea* (1873) and showed ruined columns of antiquity bathed in the elegiac light of the declining sun. A caption explained that the painting depicted 'a civilization in ruins, succumbing to the forces of nature. The crumbling buildings, overgrown with vegetation, symbolize nature's power over humanity and its structures.'

This picture was much in my mind as I drove from the Institute of Arts to the Michigan Central Railroad Station, near where the old Tigers Stadium used to be (directions in Detroit have their own special tense: everything is where something *used to be*). It occurred to me that Church's picture might have been acquired with some Dorian Grayish motive in mind – the ruination of the painted city guaranteeing the Motor City's eternal prosperity – but it ended up being an allegory or prophecy of Detroit's decline and fall, a decline and fall exemplified by the Michigan Central Railroad Station.

The station was built in 1913, a huge neoclassical edifice, fifteen or sixteen storeys high, a terminus whose function had since been terminated. The entrance was framed by Corinthian columns. Every window was broken, suggesting, somehow, that all the building's remaining energy – and it still had a lot – was spent surveying its own abandonment. I parked in front of the station and walked over to talk to a couple of people who were taking photographs.

'Oh, we're just here photographing,' said the woman, 'hoping someone would pull up and park a white car slap in the middle of the picture.'

I looked at my car. It was an unbelievably stupid place to have parked but, eager to enter into a dialogue, I said, 'Actually, I parked there entirely for your benefit.'

'You did?'

'You will recall that in Caspar David Friedrich's paintings there is usually a lone figure, a monk, say, in front of the ruined abbey or – in the most famous example – in the middle of the beach. The small figure gives a sense of focus to the fathomless longings of German Romanticism. In the case of post-industrial ruination, a human figure would be inappropriate, but a car – a white *Ford*, mind you – might be just what you need, compositionally and symbolically.'

I had come straight from the art institute and this kind of talk came quite naturally to me. While it enabled me to capture the intellectual high ground, however, I had not succeeded in regaining the lost ground of common courtesy. 'I'll tell you what,' I added. 'I'll move the car.'

When I came back the photographers were happy to take a break and tell me what had drawn them here.

'Imagine what this was like during World War Two,' said the man. 'The amount of men and equipment coming through here. The scale of the operation. The people, the cars and trucks pulling up. The trains . . .'

I tried to imagine all this commotion but could not.

'Ruins don't encourage you to dwell on what they were like in their heyday, before they were ruins,' I said. 'The Colosseum in Rome or the amphitheatre at Leptis Magna have never been anything but ruins. They're eternal ruins. It's the same here. This building could never have looked more magnificent than it does now, surrounded by its own silence. Ruins don't make you think of the past, they direct you towards the future. The effect is almost prophetic. This is what the future will end up like. This is what the future has always ended up looking like.'

If the photographers were taken aback by this display of eloquence and learning, they did not show it. They nodded as if it were perfectly natural that someone could drive up and deliver an analysis of such complexity and subtlety without so much as a by-your-leave. It was the ruins talking, of course. I was simply parroting stuff I'd written about ruins in the book I'd abandoned writing, but they weren't to know that and I was surprised they took it in their stride like this.

The station was framed and – because of the broken windows – penetrated by the sky: a specific Midwestern sky, a prairie sky, a sky at ease with hugeness, a sky that looked like it had already been round the world a couple of times, a sky with more air miles than you could ever get through. A plane cruised overhead. If I'd had a camera, I thought to myself, I would have included the plane *and* my white car in a shot of the railroad station, thereby making some kind of point about modes of transport. I almost said as much to the photographers. Instead I asked them if they knew the work of Camilo José Vergara who had himself photographed the building we were standing in front of. No, they said, they did not. This surprised me. I'd assumed they were on the Vergara trail, like me. Although I was here to cover the Detroit Electronic Music Festival, I'd arrived early so that I could see his photographs of the ruined city in the flesh (in the stone), look at the places he had looked at.

Vergara wants to preserve parts of the ruined downtown 'as an American Acropolis – that is, to allow the present skyscraper graveyard to become a park of ripe ruins'. The problem is what happens as the buildings continue to decay, when bits start falling from twenty storeys up. For Vergara that's just an administrative detail – periodic observation could identify trouble spots and fix them before people get hurt – in the larger scheme of ruination: 'the cladding of these buildings would probably take centuries to shed. In the process, ever new and surprising aspects of their semi-covered skeletons would emerge, opening perspectives right through them.' And this, he insists, is not incompatible with plans for the redevelopment of downtown, which could 'take place *around* the ruins, as it has in Rome'.

Unfortunately, this plan is 'seen by most as at best misguided and at worst a cruel joke'. Personally, I thought it an excellent idea, and my itinerary in the days leading up to the festival was largely determined by the route mapped out by Vergara's pictures. Mega ruins like the Book-Cadillac Hotel and the Statler Hilton took on the landmark importance of the Empire State Building or the Statue of Liberty for a first-time visitor to New York. Accordingly, after leaving my photographer friends – who showed signs of wanting to be left to their own devices, not lectured by a know-all they had never met before – I drove over to the old Ford plant at Highland Park. From there I drove on to Brush Park, a few blocks north of the new Tigers Stadium, just off Woodward Avenue.

In the late nineteenth century Brush Park had been the wealthiest part of the city; now it was an area of derelict Victorian mansions. Houses and the burned-out, plundered remains of houses were so thin on the ground that the area had an airy, rural quality to it. Vegetation had clambered up many of the walls – exactly as painted by Church – camouflaging them. Parked on the grass, a zebra-striped van added to the impression of a slum safari park. A mattress was crashed out on the sidewalk. Used to a life of indolence, it seemed singularly ill-equipped for living on the streets. Already soggy with rain, it looked like getting the stuffing knocked out of it in the next few days. After that it would go quickly to pieces. A few vagrants stood around fires. Smoke drifted, so did clouds. An old man levered himself along on a pair of crutches, one leg amputated at the knee. Someone else sat in a doorway, reading a newspaper with the concentration of a scholar deciphering hieroglyphics. It was a peaceful scene. Feeling as conspicuous as an investment banker, I locked my car and walked over to the corner store – George's Market – which, incredibly, was still functioning. I bought a can of Coke and stepped back outside. Half an hour earlier, at Highland Park, I'd read a plaque explaining that the first Model T Ford had come off the production line in 1913. By 1925, nine thousand Model Ts were being made in a single day, setting 'the pattern of abundance for 20th-century living'. Now, in the twenty-first century, I sat on the kerb in the Brush Park ghetto, drinking Coke, watching people pushing shopping trolleys as if the world were an enormously depleted supermarket in which there was nothing left to buy – except at George's Market, the last outpost of progress. What are those lines of Blake's (which I had come across in the Sanctuary's copy of his complete poems)? 'Wisdom is sold in the desolate market where none come to buy.' George's, though, was doing a roaring trade. People were coming and going the whole time, trading cash for bottles of 100-per-cent-proof wisdom. Except it wasn't wisdom they were getting, only its forgotten cousin, oblivion.

Beneath it all, desire of oblivion runs.

I looked at the guy straining hard over his newspaper, at another toasting his hands over a fire (it wasn't a cold day but after a certain point of dereliction you never miss a chance to warm up), and thought that I wouldn't at all mind ending up like either of them. Really, it doesn't matter much what happens to you in this life. What was there separating me and these harmless old guys? Everything and nothing. Obviously there was my hire car that I could, at any moment, drive back to the luxury of the Pontchartrain Hotel or on to the airport; from there, in terms of travel options, the sky was the limit. But if you could have taken some kind of comparative sample of the state of our souls, our hearts, I'm not sure who would have come out best.

I was feeling a bit King Leary, I suppose, sitting on the urban heath of Brush Park, but at that moment there seemed almost nothing to choose between us. Who was happier? And what gauge of a life is there other than that simple ability to be happy? 'What do they want, the people who visit the Zone?' asks the Writer in *Stalker*. 'Happiness, more than anything,' replies the Stalker. Asked which kind of people the Zone lets through, he says, 'I think that it lets those through who've lost all hope; not good or bad, but the wretched.' Our chances of getting through the Zone, then, were roughly equal. Except, as I sat there, musing on my own wretchedness, I actually felt quite happy – but that flicker of happiness was like the touch of sun on a winter's day. Step out of the sun and it's freezing and there's nothing you can do to get warm except – we've come full circle – toast your hands over a fire. Beneath this surface glow of happiness lay the cold geology – compacted, dense – of despair. I think that's why I felt content, calm. I was no longer kicking against things, straining to be happy, struggling to free myself of the unspecified weight of whatever it was – the self? – that was dragging me down. Part of me envied the sad old derelicts who had finished, utterly, with everything they had once hoped to accomplish. I would have traded places with them in an instant – except I probably wouldn't have done.

On Sunday morning – the second day of the three-day DEMF – it poured. Obviously the weather was a major downer for everyone: the organizers and performers would be affected by it more than the audience, but I found it difficult to conceive of anyone suffering from it more than me. When my girlfriend and I had split up, I had felt on the brink of a lifetime's loneliness. I no longer felt that way; I now felt I was in the *middle* of a lifetime's loneliness. My confidence was at its lowest ebb for many years. I should have been happy – I was being paid to be here – but happiness does not respond to that kind of imperative; it is no good telling yourself you should be happy.

Like anyone who travels on business I'd had high hopes, on the plane, of some kind of sexual adventure in Detroit. Circumstances could hardly have been more propitious: I was on expenses, I was staying in the Pontchartrain, a business-class hotel just over the road from a techno festival that would attract loved-up young ravers from all over the Midwest, probably America, possibly the world. I was perfectly placed. I had, in short, many things going for me but, at the same time, I had nothing going for me, and besides, several things had gone wrong in the course of the first day of the festival.

The festival was being held in the Hart Plaza, in the heart of the renovated downtown, next to the river, right across the road from the Pontchartrain, and I'd gone over there early on Saturday afternoon. Music boomed around but the plaza was deserted except for a semicircle of Porta Potties arranged in such a way – it seemed – as to grant them maximum prominence. There were a few stalls selling T-shirts, books and CDs, and a clutch of café umbrellas urging people to 'Take the Pepsi Challenge'. At the subterranean level of the plaza the food stalls were basic, unadorned, functional: a far cry from the hippy drapes, the rainbow emblems of the health food and vegan underground.

And then there was the crowd – or lack of it. At first I

wondered why the few kids slouching around were all so short. Then I realized it was because they hadn't finished growing yet. Some of them looked like they hadn't even *started* growing, and they were all wearing those unbelievable pants – as broad as they are long – that denote the candy raver in America. I did not understand these trousers: why would anyone wear pants so immense that they became a species of mutant foot-wear? You didn't wear these pants, you walked on them. Just when I'd seen the biggest, baggiest, and longest – in a word, the *phattest* – pair habitable, someone would wade by, a sail of billowing cloth on each leg. They made me feel *old*, those pants. So old, in fact, that after buying a T-shirt I went back to the Pontchartrain, where I took tea and biscuits in my room.

After that I took a ride on the People Mover, the driver-less elevated train that loops through downtown. In places the train passed within a few feet of the shattered windows and tattered awnings of abandoned hotels. I got out at Grand Circus Park, an area that seemed the epicentre of the socioeconomic earthquake that had rocked the city to its foundations. Feeling the lack of my sunglasses keenly, I walked to a spot where I could see half a dozen architecturally outstanding buildings – Kales, United Artists, Fine Arts, Park Avenue, the Statler Hilton, the Wurlitzer, the David Broderick Tower – each of them in a state of severe ruination. Having been forced out on to the streets for half a century, the weather had moved indoors, making itself at home but contributing nothing to the upkeep of the buildings.

Looking at all that vacated office space, the rust-stained concrete and boarded-up windows of vertiginous decline, I became convinced that buildings don't just fall into ruin – something in them aspires to ruination. It's the same with people. The purpose of architecture – even the most baroque, *especially* baroque – and medicine is simply to thwart the urge to collapse. (Maybe that should read 'disguise', not 'thwart'.) All we can do is keep applying the creosote, propping ourselves up with health and success, trying to keep the rain and the damp and the rot at bay for a little longer, trying to postpone the moment of complete collapse and abandonment for the same reason that one waits as long as possible for the first alcoholic drink of the day: because the longer you leave it, the better it will feel.

But even though these buildings had been abandoned, even though they were no longer fit for business, habitation, or anything else, *still* they didn't physically collapse. Until they're laid low by dynamite or wrecking balls they'll eke out some kind of existence. When all else fails they'll continue – for the lack of anything better – to stand their ground, to box their corner. Either they don't know when they're beat or force of habit – the stubbornness of memory – stops them doing anything about it.

The festival had filled up by the time I made my way back there. The Porta Potties had disappeared amid the mass of people – young and old, black and white, clubbers and squares, thin, fat and unbelievably fat – pouring into the plaza. Things had looked up so much that I became anxious – desperate in fact – to get stoned, but no one at the festival was smoking grass, presumably because of all the cops. I took a zero-tolerance attitude to this.

'A festival where you can't smoke pot,' I whined to a

sympathetic teenager, 'is not a festival, it's a trade fair.' Actually, at the Pontchartrain, I had been given a tiny amount of grass by a guy from Illinois who told me that as well as uniformed cops, there were lots of undercover cops around too. The effect of smoking this tiny amount of grass, however, was to make me want to get properly stoned and, at the same time, to make me doubly paranoid, more cautious than ever. I walked around in the yellow, social realist MADE IN DETROIT T-shirt that I had bought earlier in the day, looking for people smoking grass. If I saw anyone doing anything vaguely discreet I drew near and tried to see if they were smoking pot, but no one ever was, and this only made me more desperate to find people who were. Most people were dancing but I was paying no attention to the music and was focusing all my concentration on sniffing out people who were smoking grass. A woman with peroxide hair returned my scrutiny with open contempt. A few minutes later, a kid in a Plastikman T-shirt glared at me with equal hostility. Considering it was a festival, people weren't very friendly . . .

Then the penny dropped. More accurately, it plummeted: I was acting like an undercover cop. Intent on finding people smoking grass, I was patrolling the crowd like a narc. This realization reredoubled my paranoia and I felt even more conspicuous (especially since I did not have my sunglasses to hide behind), alienated and ill at ease. I tried to lose myself in the music but I was not able to cast off my new, unwanted identity so easily. Behind my back, I was sure people were pointing me out to their friends, warning them that the guy in the brand-new MADE IN DETROIT T-shirt, the one pretending to dance, the thin guy with grey hair, was a narc.

Stacey Pullen played the final set of that first night of the festival, sampling Martin Luther King's 'Now is the time' speech, but now was not the time for me, if it ever had been, and I felt it never would be. It was all utterly momentous, a moment of historic importance, in fact (King had given a version of that speech, here in Detroit, in 1963, months before the canonical March on Washington), but I was standing to one side, apart from the moment rather than a part of it. The crowd was ecstatic but it all felt – to the outsider I had now become – like Nuremberg on E. I was actually relieved when the festival closed for the day and we all began pouring out of the Hart Plaza.

At the Pontchartrain – which normally would be full of besuited automobile executives – the elevators were crammed with DJs, ravers, hipsters: the variously dilated peoples coming back to their rooms before going on to after-parties in clubs or in one another's rooms. It was probably the hippest gathering in any hotel ever and I was missing out on it completely even though I was there. I went back to my room and lay on my king-size bed, drinking beer, watching Debbie do Dallas with the sound turned down so the people in the next room (whom I later heard having sex) would not hear. If you are happy, being alone in a hotel – on expenses, drinking beer and watching porno – is close to bliss; but if you are lonely and unloved it is utterly soul-destroying. Even though what I was seeing – things going in and out of other things in depilated close-up – was real in the sense that it was actually happening, the aesthetic was so implausible (blondes in stockings and heels, with red nails and breasts the size of small balloons) that any human contact seemed contrived, false, unattainable.

Not that that stopped me watching. No, that's what *kept* me watching. I will never have sex again, I thought to myself, and part of the reason I felt that was because I was watching porno – but, since I was never going to have sex again, there was nothing to stop me watching it: a form of self-mortifying solace.

I woke up on Sunday morning feeling even more desolate than I had when – without even jerking off – I'd eventually fallen asleep. I drew back the curtains and saw that it was bucketing down. The hotel was utterly silent. I was the only person in the place who was awake so early. Everyone else was still in bed, sleeping off the after-effects of the after-parties they'd been to after the festival. The idea of breakfast at the hotel was too depressing to contemplate. As I made my way through the deserted lobby a young couple in T-shirts and flares walked in – smiling and calm, wide-eyed, glowing. I left the hotel and drove through the industrial rain to the Clique, a diner about a mile down Jefferson.

Like George's Market, the Clique was doing a roaring trade. People were chewing like fury and the staff were working flat out to keep them fed. It was a car plant of nutrition, the Clique, turning out an endless quantity of good, no-frills body fuel. Even though it was crowded, I ended up in a booth for four, thereby duplicating the excess of solitude – two king-size beds – of my hotel room. The busboy came and wiped the table.

'How ya doin'?' he said.

'I'm bound upon a wheel of fire that mine own tears do scald like molten lead,' I said. 'Apart from that I'm fine. How're *you* doing?'

'I'm doin' fine.' He grinned, making a really good job of wiping the table. At some point the American emphasis on money – do your job well or we'll get somebody else to do it for you – meets the Buddhist idea of performing a task well not for any financial reward but simply to do justice to the task. So it doesn't matter if your job is simply to clear away greasy plates and wipe tables – you wipe that table for all you are worth (about $6.50 an hour) as if your life depended on it.

Rain was blurring past the window and I was sitting in my booth, looking at the rain, slurping weak coffee. I was also reading the local paper, the *Detroit Free Press*, full of news about the festival which looked like being severely compromised by the rain. My food arrived. The eggs were runny, the bacon crisp, the hash browns excellent but, notwithstanding this, I was in a state of the most utter dejection. I was in a state of such abject despair that I was, in a sense, oblivious to it.

It was raining outside. Not a howling storm, just steady drizzle. The kind of rain that yields no sense of when it might ease up, that seems to be keeping itself in reserve so that it can, if necessary, keep going till the end of time. 'It was raining outside.' Gore Vidal derides someone for writing a sentence like that, feigning surprise or relief that it was not raining *in*side. But that day in the Clique I looked down and saw that it *was* raining inside as well as outside. My egg-smeared plate was becoming wet. Drops of water were falling on to my toast, moistening my eggy hash browns. As I looked it rained harder and I could not see. I was crying. Not sobbing, just this steady leak of tears. And then, as I realized I was crying, I felt that I was in danger of sobbing. I got a grip on myself, stopped the leak, staunched it. I ate my wet eggs and looked at the rain outside, hoping that would take my mind off the rain inside. I'm having a breakdown, I said to myself, I'm having a breakdown while having breakfast. I said this to myself to calm myself down, to try to familiarize and render ordinary the extraordinary turn of events that had led to this internal rain. I stifled my sobs and ate my breakfast which did not taste any worse because I was having a nervous breakdown. When I had finished the eggs I wiped my knife with a napkin and spread butter and apricot jelly on the wholewheat toast. I finished the rest of my coffee. I calmed down. I was no longer leaking tears but I was no less distraught now than when I was having a nervous breakdown, which I was still having even though I had, to a degree, managed to regain control of myself.

The weather outside was also clearing but I decided not to go to the festival until later in the afternoon. I went for a drive instead. Another car was pulling out of the Clique's parking lot and I followed it unthinkingly for several miles, simply because I liked the bumper sticker: PAVE THE RAIN FOREST. Paying no attention to where I was going, I found solace in the simple act of driving, of seeing buildings that were in an even worse state than I was. Watching porno makes you very aware that you're watching what you're meant to do or have, that it's *you* sitting watching it; but when you're driving a car you are just a guy driving a car. It makes no difference who you are; you could be anyone – which suited me fine since the person I least wanted to be was me.

I ended up in an area south of Interstate 94, east of 75.

I didn't know what this area – you couldn't call it a neighbourhood – was called; possibly it wasn't called anything. There were Vergara ruins everywhere, spread out, intermingling the rustic and the industrial. At one point I found myself next to a bricked-up warehouse – Hoban Foods – on Warren, just east of Riopelle Street. Near by was a cold-storage plant, a water tower and another warehouse, still in some kind of use. Most of the other places had subsided into uselessness and housed nothing but air; they had the form of warehouses but none of the contents. In the middle distance were two church spires and, beyond them, the gleaming skyscape of the renovated downtown. Grass was grazing wherever it could. It had stopped raining, the sky was already blue in places. There were even a few trees. The road was crossed by a rusting railroad track, running north–south. Against the blue of the sky the faded red of the crossing sign could be read as a caption or title, but it is not just its place in the history of American painting, film, and photography that gives the empty railroad crossing its special resonance. There was something elemental about this meeting of rail and road.

When you come upon a railroad crossing in the emptiness of the Midwest there is a pleasing sense of the hugeness of a continent manifesting itself in a single spot. You might be lost but you feel you are at the exact centre point of the compass. It's not just that road and rail intersect; the meeting of those two purpose-driven ribbons is so contrary to the directionless emptiness that you succumb simultaneously to a sense of enormous expansion and of intense convergence.

In a busy city, if the railroad is in use and you are in a hurry, it's frustrating having to wait for an interminable freight to rumble by. But here, on a road without traffic, surrounded by abandoned industrial buildings, faced with a railroad on which trains no longer ran, I was happy to wait, to pull over, to park and walk around. I stopped because it felt as if time too was lapsing, in the process of stopping. Maybe that's why it felt filmic, almost photograph-like. If I'd looked far enough down the tracks perhaps I could have seen the last train that had passed by years earlier, the rails rusting in its wake. But I didn't, or at least not for long enough. Time, like the train, had moved on. The present had already turned into the past. That's why the spot had this gravitational stillness. And I was not the first person to have responded to it and stopped here: right by the wheel of my car I could see a small pile of ciga-rette butts that someone, evidently, had emptied out from the ashtray of their car.

My mood had improved markedly. I was looking forward to returning to the Pontchartrain, to the festival, to filling my head with hours of bangin' techno, to not acting like a narc, but for the moment I had no urge to be anywhere – or do anything – else. I liked it here. I was happy where I was.

All around was a litter-strewn acreage of parking lots and railroad tracks. Lying near my feet was an old can of Coke which, when I kicked it, turned out to be full, unopened. A freight of clouds moved towards the horizon. A rusted sign was still doing its best to admonish:

NO PARK N   IN
BAC   O
C RB

At the base of the sign a thicket of tough grass had taken hold. In almost every crack in the concrete there was a sprouting of grey-green grass: the prairie making a slow comeback.

THE ZONE

In a well-known flight of more than fancy, Coleridge reflected on dreams and their aftermath. Suppose 'a man could pass through Paradise in a dream, and have a flower presented to him as a pledge that his soul had really been there'. And if, when he awoke, he found petals in his hand? 'What then?' Coleridge wondered.

What then?

On a dark afternoon in February 2000 I was getting ready to fly to Manila. I took out of the cupboard my faded grey shorts that I'd last worn in Nevada the previous September. Before stuffing them in my rucksack I checked through all the pockets, hoping to come across a stash of forgotten, laundered dollars. There was no money, the pockets were empty – except for a few greasy, pink, synthetic feathers.

In the summer of 1990 an announcement in a San Francisco newsletter proposed a 'Zone Trip' into 'the unknown'. Eighty-nine people met at the baseball diamond in Golden Gate Park and drove through the night to the Black Rock Desert in Nevada. In the morning they were confronted with an expanse of flat, white emptiness. To say that there were mountains or hills in the distance makes no sense, for everything here is in the distance. The playa is pure distance.

Someone drew a long line in the playa and said, 'On the other side of this line everything is different.' Then the eighty-nine participants held hands and stepped over the line, into the Zone.

The people who made that trip in 1990 had with them only a few props: a generator to power the movie projector for a screening of *Bad Day at Black Rock*, a sound system and costumes for the cocktail party that would precede the burning of the wooden figure of a man, a single neon sign, water, a little shelter. If the environment overwhelmed the senses, it also served as an irresistible incentive to the imagination. Suggestive of limitless creativity, the infinite flatness of the playa was mirrored at night by the star-clogged sky. The sublime emptiness of the desert raised the possibility of not just staging a spectacle but creating a visionary reality. People fell to thinking what they would do when they came back the following year.

Accordingly, in 1991, when they and others returned, the empty space was dotted with small theme camps: Christmas Camp, English Safari Camp . . . Each year this community – and the scale of its imaginative ambitions – grew until, by the time I first made the trip ten years later, it had become a city: Black Rock City, with a temporary population of twenty-five thousand.

For fifty-one weeks of the year an aerial photograph of the Black Rock Desert would show . . . nothing. Apart from the weather, anything that happened here happened tens of millions of years ago – except, that could not be more wrong. For one week of the year a picture of the same area would show a city rivalling Las Vegas in the intensity and extravagance of its lights. For one week of the year it becomes the most visible place on the planet, as fantastical as one of Calvino's invisible cities. And then it is gone. Once again there is just the endless expanse of desert. No trace of it remains – except in the hearts and minds of its citizens, dispersed around the globe.

Black Rock City is often termed a Temporary Autonomous Zone. Hakim Bey's subversive idea of the TAZ – 'an uprising which does not engage directly with the State, a guerrilla operation which liberates an area (of land, of time, of imagination) and then dissolves itself to re-form elsewhere/elsewhen *before* the State can crush it' – is *nowhere* more deliriously realized than at Black Rock City. I mean this quite literally. The 'Welcome to Nowhere' signs at Burning Man implicitly hyphenate the word, admitting you to Now-*here*, *Now*-here.

Asked what she believes, a character in Robert Stone's *Damascus Gate* replies, 'I believe in liberation. That if it's possible for me, it's possible for everyone. And I won't have mine until everyone does.' Bey is contemptuous of this kind of dialectical postponement. 'To say that "I will not be free till all humans (or all sentient creatures) are free" is simply to cave in to a kind of nirvana stupor, to abdicate our humanity, to define ourselves as losers.' It is more important for a few people to achieve liberation for a while, *now* and *here*.

A site of 'unmediated creativity', the TAZ offers 'a peak experience on the social as well as individual scale'. Bey goes on to imagine a 'whole new geography, a kind of pilgrimage map in which holy sites are replaced by peak experiences and TAZs'.

Oh, but the holy sites – Preah Kahn, Borobodur, Wat Khao Phanom Phloeng – can be the sites of peak experience too. And it is precisely their permanence, the sense that one is in a place where time has stood its ground, that gives them their power.

Wat Phra That Doi Suthep is perched on a mountain ten miles out of Chiang Mai. A cloud of red bougainvillaea drifted above a tiled terrace which seemed, in turn, to float over the smog-shrouded city. Incense was burning. A row of candles waxed lyrical in the daylight. Next to them was a gold Buddha on which visitors stuck squares of gold leaf that flickered in the breeze. As they came partially unstuck they glinted and twisted in the sunlight, sometimes floating completely free. The smoke from the candles and incense made it seem that the Buddha was flickering into golden flame.

On the other side of the world, in the Black Rock Desert, a statue to a non-specific deity had been built. Here, too, people attached little pieces of paper on which they'd written messages. By the time I got there the shape of the statue had become blurred by the thick accumulation of words. Unable to think of anything to write, I copied out some lines of Auden's:

May I, composed . . .
Of Eros and of dust,
Beleaguered by the same
Negation and despair,
Show an affirming flame.

After pasting on these borrowed words I wandered the
playa until I came to a place where a small crowd had gathered. A young man was suspended in a Perspex container of
water. He was breathing – in the middle of the desert – through
an Aqua-Lung. A fairground barker addressed the crowd
through a megaphone, pitching the redemption offered by
Waterboy. Painted blue, naked except for a ten-gallon hat – in
the aquatic circumstances, it was a perfectly appropriate form
of dress – a supplicant went and stood in front of Waterboy,
who was bubbling away like a human bong.

'Do you renounce the dryness?' called the megaphone
apostle.

'Yes,' responded the would-be convert.

'What do you renounce?'

'The dryness.'

'Do you embrace the wetness?'

'Yes.'

'What do you love?'

'I am in love with moistness.'

'Come forward and kneel.' As he did so some kind of
valve opened, anointing him with water from Waterboy's altar.

'Now you are moist. Go forth,' said the apostle. 'Who
else is ready to renounce the dryness?'

I got distracted by so much other stupid shit like this

that it was dark by the time I made my way back to the statue on which I'd glued those words of Auden's. If there'd been any kind of ceremony, I'd missed it. As I got near, the statue was already flickering into flame. Some of the pieces of paper came loose as they caught fire and drifted into the desert sky like burning leaves. Within minutes the whole thing was a mass of golden flame, filling the eyes of everyone there.

The TAZ, for Bey, is a 'republic of gratified desires'; in keeping with this, a friend once described Burning Man as a place where everyone can become whatever they want to be. It was, we agreed, the sexiest, the most glamorous, the funnest, the kindest, the wildest, the politest, the freest – add the superlatives of your choice, they're bound to be appropriate – place on earth: a place where all your dreams can come true. And still, he said in amazement – there were tears in his eyes as he spoke – there were people who didn't believe in it, who didn't want to come!

The Zone in Tarkovsky's *Stalker* is a place where 'your most cherished desire will come true'. Near the end of the film, on his return from the Zone, the Stalker is distraught because all people care about is 'how to get a higher price, how to get paid for every breath they take . . . they don't believe in anything'. Ultimately, of course, this makes no difference: visited or not, the Zone – 'the quietest place on earth' – is *still there*.

I set my alarm for six and walked to the ruins of the ancient city of Si Satchanalai in the still-warm almost-darkness. As I approached Wat Chang Lom, the greyness began to take on a hint of colour. The Buddha images surrounding the central *chedi* were all broken in some way: one lacked a hand, another a head; in the most extreme cases only a residue of grace suggested that the stone had once been coaxed into a likeness of the Buddha. Rilke's 'Archaic Torso of Apollo' admonished: 'You must change your life.' These ruined Buddhas admonish no one but they reminded me of something Brodsky wrote: 'One is changed by what one loves.' Brodsky was consciously changing Auden's several permutations of this sentiment. In 1933 Auden had suggested that 'men are changed by what they do'; the *New Year Letter* of 1940 supplemented this with the idea that 'we are changed by what we change'; ten years later, in 'In Transit', he made the more elaborate claim that

> Somewhere are places where we have really been,
>   dear spaces
>   Of our deeds and faces, scenes we remember
> As unchanging because there we changed . . .

I walked up the worn steps of a low hill to the ruins of Wat Khao Phanom Phloeng. A tangle of forest and grey-green fields sloped clear of the mist that obscured much of the surrounding lowland. The air was full of the hoot and whistle, the shriek of waking birds, but nothing moved. The stillness deepened with every step. It was like approaching the source of all the calm in the world. Passing behind two denuded *chedis* I saw the back of a huge seated Buddha, draped with an orange sash, facing the sun as it poured flaming red through the trees.

* * *

We had been up all night, were cycling home across the playa. The night had not been without its disappointments and difficulties. We had failed to make the finals of the Great Canadian Beaver-Eating Contest. An Afrika Korps sandstorm had swept through the desert while we were way out on the playa, miles from any shelter. The wind had subsided after that and we had spent the rest of the night at Space Cowboys and Bianca's.

A little while earlier two neon kangaroos had bounced past in the star-splashed darkness, but the night was fading quickly now. We stopped to take a look at a submarine – the HMS *Love* – breaking the surface of the desert floor. It was too cold to stay long and so we got on our bikes again. I was wearing a pink fluoro boa which, in the way of all scarves, became entangled in the derailleur. My bicycle stopped in its tracks.

'Your boa has constricted itself,' said Sarah (who had come full circle and was no longer calling herself Circle). Disentangling it did not take long and, except for a few grease-smeared tufts which I pocketed, my feather boa was only slightly the worse for this traumatic wear. We rode towards our camp but stopped again when we came to the Man.

'The Man is so silent, isn't he?' said Sarah, a remark all the more astute for being so obvious. A towering skeletal structure of wood and – at night – coloured neon, the Man is the epicentre and focus of everything that happens here. Himself an emblem of the event, representations of the Man are endlessly replicated across Black Rock City. Near our tent a lanky pink wind-sock Man danced, flame-like, in the desert wind. En route from San Francisco we'd seen several cars on whose dusty windows the simple symbol of the Man had been drawn: two steeply crossed lines intersecting two-thirds of the way along their length – legs, trunk, and arms – with a simple triangle for a head. The day before, Sarah had painted a long, etiolated version on my back. Underneath, so that people would know who I was, she wrote my name in Day-Glo red: THIN MAN.

The sky was violet-tinged, growing light. Red-eyed, already boiling, the sun climbed over the distant mountains, silhouetting the Man, covering us in a vast lattice-shadow of ribs and legs.

Freud's 'flight of imagination' about Rome in *Civilization and Its Discontents* tempts me into another. If successive phases of history can be imagined as sharing a common space, then perhaps, by analogy, chronologically distinct experiences of certain places – Rome, Detroit, Leptis Magna, Amsterdam, New Orleans – also occur in some ways simultaneously. If the successive can be experienced simultaneously, then perhaps distance can be experienced as immanence. They might be tied to specific locations but, in 'the sphere of the mind', some experiences – separated, originally, by years as well as miles – end up sharing a single location and a single instant. Everything happens at the same time and in the same place – or certain things, certain experiences do at any rate. Instead of chronology, narrative or story, there is an endless accretion – a kind of negative archaeology – of material. There is still suspense (in fact, there is nothing but suspense) but there is no next.

As I sit here writing, Wat Khao Phanom Phloeng is still there, where it was, where it's been for hundreds of years. And if it's still there, then I'm still there too. The only way to prove this, of course, is by going back there. If I *did* go back I would find myself sitting there, or wandering around, sipping water from a bottle, making unintelligible notes. What would have changed in the meantime? From the Buddha's point of view, nothing. From mine, nothing.

From this I conclude that the temporary city of Black Rock is still there, and that I'm still there too . . .

Why? Because those lines of Auden's from 'Detective Story' suddenly make perfect sense: because it's *my* home.

Black Rock City always takes the form of a giant horseshoe, from two till ten on a topographical clock face with the Man the still point around which the hands – had there been any – would turn. With the spatial defined by the temporal like this, you always know exactly where you are. Lamps mark a half-mile-long avenue stretching across the playa from Centre Camp (six o'clock) to the Man. In daylight, this avenue of extinguished lamps is both reminiscent of the Via Sacra of the Forum in Rome and suggestive of a future archaeology: the blueprint of a civilization briefly glimpsed. Just before dusk every day the lamps are lit, with some solemnity, by a small procession of lamplighters. Burning Man is usually associated with the primal abandon of the night of the Burn, but this ceremonial lighting of lamps honours a different kind of flame: the steady, ongoing fire of civilization.

The sun had just set. The lamps of Black Rock City were being lit. We were at our camp, preparing for the chill of night, stitching El-wire on to our coats, when excited whoops and yells spread through the city. Tammy and John were on top of their RV, calling us to come up. The cries and shouts were growing louder all the time. From the roof of the RV we could see the city spreading out for miles. Off to the north-east was the endless expanse of the playa. Directly east was a range of mountains and, in the dim blue above them, the huge silver disc of the risen moon.

The bus from Luang Prabang to Vang Vieng twisted through high jungle, much of which we could not see. It was the beginning of the rainy season and for most of the journey the mountains were shrouded with cloud. Occasionally the sun blazed out and the jungle reared up in the distance where we had thought there was nothing but mist and rain and sky.

After a couple of hours we stopped for lunch at the small town of Kasi. We got off the bus and looked around even though there wasn't much to look at. Actually, the things most worth looking at turned out to be us: dozens of children ran up just to look and laugh and say a few hilariously friendly words. It was so humid it felt like it was raining. A butterfly landed on the kerb nearby, its dull wings closed vertically together. One of the little boys who had thronged around us pointed to it and smiled and we smiled back – yes, butterfly! – even though it, like Kasi, wasn't worth looking at. Then the boy moved his hand closer and the butterfly opened its wings which were a saturated, almost-black blue. On each of them were a bright silver moon and splashes of distant stars. The butterfly closed its wings, showing once more the dull brown of their undersides. The boy moved his hands again and we had another glimpse of blue, star-drenched space. It was like an image transmitted back to earth from *Voyager* or the Hubble: a map of the cosmos printed on a tiny creature's wings.

Who can remember that mad night when the Man burned? You don't *remember* it, it's more like your head is still aflame with the experience. Part of you is still there, part of you is waiting for it to happen again. For five days and nights we had been in the desert and the Man was always there, silent, not judging, and then, on the Saturday, there was a conflagration. The sky was traversed by green lasers that made me think I was indoors at a club. At the same time I also thought the lights in the distance – the lights of camps at the other side of Black Rock City – were the outskirts of Vegas. I elided these two thoughts by thinking I was in a gigantic club called the Outskirts of Vegas. A neon butterfly flapped through the darkness, followed by a school of El-wire cod. A comet or meteor shower passed a couple of hundred feet overhead and the Man started to burn. Suddenly everything was a *Hindenburg* of flame and everyone went completely mad. Sarah said, 'Would you say the Man was engulfed by flames?' and I felt the word 'engulfed' had never been used quite so aptly. In fact, everywhere was engulfed by flames and there were naked people everywhere, charging round the flames, and everything was suddenly engulfed by everything else, even the desert, which was engulfed by the overarching firmament which was all-engulfing. It was like the end of the world except it was like the beginning of the world.

The next day a stunned silence hung over the playa. Already people were leaving, the city starting to disappear. Twenty-four hours from now it would be gone. Only the desert would remain. I walked out on to the playa. Where the Man had stood there were now only ashes and smouldering embers. People were throwing a few things into the ashes. I remembered something I had read years ago – 'Burn what you have worshipped, worship what you have burned' – and, for the third or fourth time that week, found myself in tears. They were tears of recognition: that I had reached some frontier of what I was capable of. Even as it felt like I was accessing this new part of myself, however, I remembered other occasions – on my first visit to the cemeteries of the Somme, for example – when I had come to some previous high point of my life. So why were these embers moving me so deeply?

Nothing I had ever experienced had brought home to me as forcibly as Burning Man that fundamental truth which is so easy to know, so hard to live by: giving is getting. Because nothing is sold at Black Rock City, people often assume that bartering takes the place of cash. But barter, really, is just a less efficient method of exchange. At Burning Man something very different – a gift economy – is at work. Life, it is often said, is a matter of give and take. Yes, but at its highest level life should be a matter of giving and giving. Years later, in Bali, I visited the Ubud Sari Health Resort. It was set up by someone whose name I can't remember. Not that it matters; but what I do remember is something written on the plaque that was dedicated to his memory: 'No one ever became poor through giving.' At Black Rock City everyone becomes rich by giving.

But that was not the only reason why these embers had affected me so powerfully. For much of that year, TV news bulletins had been dominated by images of smouldering ashes: houses in Kosovo burned down in the name of the long-held grievances of rabid nationalism. The homes of ethnic Albanians were the first to go, torched by marauding Serbs, followed, months later, by Serbian homes set ablaze by ethnic Albanians bent on revenge. On the one hand, then, fires suggesting that the idea of progress, of an ameliorative version of history, lay in ashes; on the other, here in the desert, embers suggesting what civilization could still become.

In Si Satchanalai that morning I'd made my way round to the front of the Buddha at Wat Khao Phanom Phloeng. The sun was still burning red through the trees. The air was full of the sound of birds. The Buddha exuded such serenity that I had an impulse to fall to my knees. I resisted it, but what can you do when you are profoundly moved? There is only a limited repertoire of gestures available to us in moments like these. What might take their place? Are there new gestures, new ways of articulating our need for grace and beauty?

Nietzsche wondered what buildings might be suitable for contemplation and thought in the godless age he had prophetically announced. Churches? No, they were all clammy with Christianity. It is the same with a gesture like kneeling: it's tainted. I didn't kneel but I didn't know what to do instead. The sun was there, the Buddha was there, and I stood there, too, quietly, trying to quell the chatter of thoughts in my head. My head was still full of Nietzsche who claimed that prayer was invented to give stupid people something to do with their hands, to stop them fidgeting and creating a disturbance. Perhaps, in sacred sites, this is the function of the modern camera: to give you something to do with your hands. I didn't have a camera, of course; all I could do was *be there*.

But perhaps the attitudes of prayer are not so easily discarded. Looking at the serene old Buddha, I remembered how, in the midst of the prolonged and desolate period of my life that I have mentioned earlier, consumed by disappointment and regret, unable to make any progress with anything, I had found myself on the tube to King's Cross. I was heading to a party I'd been looking forward to for weeks, but by the time I got as far as Pimlico, I dreaded being there and wanted only to return home, to be on my own. I got out, crossed the platform, and took the next train back south. And then, at Stockwell, the thought of being in my flat seemed so terrible that I once again got on a train heading north. This pattern repeated itself at several stations on the Victoria line. A psychiatrist monitoring the CCTV footage would have concluded that I was on the brink of throwing myself under one of these trains. Instead I kept getting on and getting off until eventually – by this time I had succeeded in getting as far north as Warren Street – I got enough of a grip on myself to get on a southbound train, shut my eyes, and stay on it. As the train hurtled through the tunnel I opened my eyes and glimpsed myself in the darkness of the opposite window. Intent only on holding myself together, on getting myself back home, with no thought of God or any kind of salvation other than that offered by my flat (TV, sofa, beer), I had assumed the classic attitude of prayer. My hands were locked together in front of my face, my head was bowed. To anyone else I must have looked devout, at peace even.

And here I was now, staring at the embers where the

Man had stood. It was a high point in my life but it also felt familiar: one of those moments that make your whole life seem worthwhile because it has led to this, to this moment. Given a choice, I'd have lived my whole life over again quite happily, changing nothing. Even catching chlamydia from Angela in New Orleans, or losing my sunglasses (which, at that time, I had not yet lost and was confident – I was *wearing* them! – of never losing), and the bits that I couldn't remember (which were still to come). Some kind of offering had to be made. And so – the ludicrousness of the gesture made it all the more fitting – I placed my pink feather boa on the embers and watched it turn, slowly, into flame.

The Buddha images at Wat Chetupon, near Sukothai, are all the more striking for being in such poor condition. They are like X-rays, still in the process of being made, of time itself. The left arm of the walking Buddha vanishes just above the elbow; below the knee, the right leg exists only as a tendon attached to a large Giacometti foot. It is no more than the ghost of a statue, so faded, so worn, that, like Francesca Woodman in one of her photographs, the Buddha seems to be stepping out of – or disappearing into – the wall that supports and frames him.

Just before the Man was completely engulfed in flame, one of his knees gave way. He lurched forwards and it looked, for a moment, as if he were about to step clear of the fire that defined and claimed him.

NOTES

There are, obviously, some unacknowledged (mis)quotations in the text. Here are the less obvious ones.

p. 112. 'as blue as the most exploded tradition': Henry James, *Italian Hours*.

p. 117. 'Noon-time's stupor' and 'the month of stalled pendulums': Joseph Brodsky, 'Roman Elegies', *To Urania*.

p. 118. 'a time that has died': Marguerite Yourcenar, 'Reflections on the Composition of *Memoirs of Hadrian*'.

p. 175. 'cold as the sea . . .': Rebecca West, *Black Lamb and Grey Falcon*.

p. 180. 'Every archway was a picture . . .': Henry James on the Claudian Aqueduct near Rome, *Italian Hours*.

p. 193. Virginia Woolf on 'the brightest thing in nature': I take Michael Hofmann's word for it – 'Summer', *Approximately Nowhere*.

p. 207. 'Beneath it all, desire of oblivion runs': Philip Larkin, 'Wants'.

p. 235. 'Burn what you have worshipped . . .': Saint Remi, quoted by Roland Barthes, *The Responsibility of Forms*.

p. 61. Gregor is quoting from Rilke's 'Dove That Ventured Outside':

Ah the ball that we hurled into infinite space,
doesn't it fill our hand differently with its return:
heavier by the weight of where it has been.

A NOTE ON THE TYPE

Goudy Old Style was designed by Frederic W. Goudy in 1915. It is a graceful, slightly eccentric typeface, and is prized by book designers for its elegance and readability.

Inspired by William Morris' Arts and Crafts movement, Frederic Goudy designed over ninety typefaces throughout his career, and is one of the most influential American type designers of the twentieth century.

GEOFF DYER
WHITE SANDS

From the author of
YOGA FOR PEOPLE WHO CAN'T BE BOTHERED TO DO IT

Experiences from the Outside World

'Brilliant . . . Dyer's eyes miss nothing'
Peter Conrad, *Observer*

'An examination of some of the fundamental
questions of life . . . Inspiring and informing'
Guardian

CANON▮▮GATE

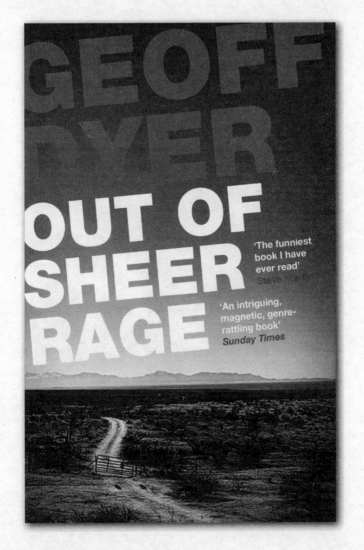

'The funniest
book I have
ever read'
Steve March

'An intriguing,
magnetic, genre-
rattling book'
Sunday Times

'The kind of book that gives literary criticism
a bad name. Hilarious!' John Berger

CANON▌GATE

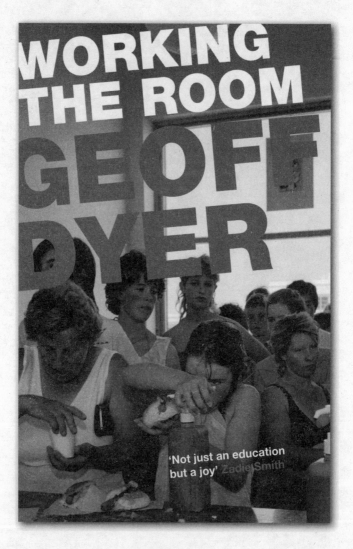

'Not just an education but a joy' Zadie Smith

'Shrewd, funny, original . . . very good company
on the page' Andrew Motion, *Guardian*

CANON█GATE